A Parent's Guide to
Coaching Basketball

John P. McCarthy, Jr.

BETTERWAY BOOKS
Cincinnati, Ohio

A Parent's Guide to Coaching Basketball. Copyright © 1990 by John P. McCarthy, Jr. Printed and bound in the United States of America. All rights reserved. No part of this book may be reproduced in any form or by any electronic or mechanical means including information storage and retrieval systems without permission in writing from the publisher, except by a reviewer, who may quote brief passages in a review. Published by Betterway Books, an imprint of F&W Publications, Inc., 1507 Dana Avenue, Cincinnati, Ohio 45207. 1-800-289-0963. First edition.

96 95 94   5 4

Library of Congress Cataloging-in-Publication Data

McCarthy, John P., 1947-
A parent's guide to coaching basketball / by John P. McCarthy.
        p.   cm.
    Includes index.
    ISBN 1-55870-170-2
    1. Basketball for children--Coaching.   I. Title.
GV886.25.M37 1990
796.323'2--dc20   90-38105
                                                          CIP

Betterway Books are available at special discounts for sales promotions, premiums and fund-raising use. Special editions or book excerpts can also be created to specification. For details contact: Special Sales Director, Betterway Books, 1507 Dana Avenue, Cincinnati, Ohio 45207.

To Mom and Dad.
My best friends, my champions.
With Love.

PREFACE

"Dad, I'd really like to get a lot of playing time next year, maybe even start in some varsity games." I could see how serious my son Jack was. He had played some basketball in grammar school. However, he did not make the freshman team in high school. As a sophomore, he was given a chance. He began to show his ability, and got good "playing time" on the J.V. team. Unfortunately, halfway through the season he slipped while rebounding and broke his wrist.

He really wanted to contribute to his team next year, but he also knew he needed to improve a lot, and to make up somehow for lost experience. "Okay," I said, "Let's go for it. I'll coach you this summer." I had played the game my whole life, and knew I could help develop his skills. It worked out great! Jack made a major improvement and I had the best parenting and coaching experience of my life.

It was the summer of 1984. We worked nearly every day. At first, we concentrated on dribbling, and practiced a lot of jump shots. We played a lot of one-on-one to refine his offensive and defensive skills. Our family took a four week trip across country that summer. The girls would groan as we spotted a basketball court on a prairie in South Dakota and pulled over for a quick forty-five minutes of practice. We practiced once in 110 degree heat in Texas!

I would start under the basket and feed him rebounds for 10-15 foot jumpers until his arms nearly fell off. He would dribble with eyes closed, speed dribble 30 yard dashes, jump rope, pass against a wall at a close distance, and shoot fouls until he was exhausted.

That year no one could believe his improvement! He played a lot, and started some varsity games by the end of the season. This is a boy who was cut as a freshman! What's my point? *A parent can make a difference!*

You don't need to be a former (or current) basketball player. It helps, but it's not necessary. This book will teach you all you need to know. Even if you are not athletically inclined, you can have a catch, feed rebounds, and be a companion to your child. This book will show you what to look for, how to spot errors in form. Most important, this book will focus on concepts, so you and your child can understand the *why* of things.

I also coached my younger son in a clinic program for beginners. There I learned a lot about what kids need to do before they can be competitive. Remember, 85% of kids who play in grammar school or clinics will never play for their high school team. But, if they learn the game, they will play in lots and playgrounds for their whole lives. Get your child just to hang in there until he learns the basics, and he will play this wonderful game for the rest of his life.

It's all here in this book. I have presented it in a way that a parent who knows little about the game can nonetheless understand the concepts. I focus on those things that can *most quickly* improve your child's chances to get some quality playing time. Moreover, the book also includes a full technical review of the game, and thus is useful also for youth coaches and players. Good luck with it.

To Kids
Jack McCarthy

CONTENTS

1.
DRIBBLING

THE IMPORTANCE OF DRIBBLING

The most important skill in youth basketball is dribbling, so it follows that the most important thing you can do as a parent coach is to teach and emphasize this to your child. How often do we see a youngster out on a basketball playground, standing there shooting, just shooting and nothing else?

Sure, shooting is important. Passing is even more important to team success. However, dribbling is a purely individual skill, and it is the most important initial step in the development of a young basketball player. *It is definitely the best confidence builder.* A boy or girl who can move with the basketball will be valuable to the team, and also will be able to develop other skills more quickly.

Children typically begin playing basketball in clinic-type programs for a few years prior to fifth or sixth grade when regular traveling teams are formed. Observe these programs and you'll quickly notice that confusion reigns on the court. Few shots are taken because the ball is constantly being stolen. A child will get the ball and just *freeze*. He will be immediately surrounded by opposing players, and will either throw the ball away or have it swiped from his hands. The standout on the floor is the child who does not freeze, but *who can dribble* the ball around the other players. This child can then advance for a good shot, or pass the ball to an open teammate. Thus, confidence grows, all skills become developed,

Figure 1
PRACTICE DRIBBLING

Set up cones and dribble in the cellar

Between the legs, behind the back, just fool around

and a basketball player emerges. Dribbling is the ticket! When children lack this skill, they are somewhat afraid of the ball. You can see they don't *want* the ball, and they lack confidence when they have it. Practice dribbling to address this problem and the result will be a bounty of self assurance.

So, as a parent, get your child to work on dribbling and handling the ball. When my youngest son was eight years old, I cleared out a small area in the basement (it's cold outside during basketball season in New Jersey), a space of about 10' x 10'. Even a smaller space is okay. He would go down for twenty minutes and practice dribbling. I told him to make sudden moves, perform figure eights, dribble behind the back, set up obstacles and dribble around them, and also practice dribbling with both hands. (See Figure 1.) After a while, I would put some pressure on him, try to steal the ball. We set up a runway between cellar rooms so he would get some speed

Figure 2
DRIBBLE WITH THE FINGERS

*Let the fingers and upper
palm do the dribbling*

*Keep the ball out on the
fingers as much as possible*

for a 20 foot speed dribble. In a very short time he improved signifi-
cantly, and the improvement was quite noticeable as he played in
the clinic. Don't expect miracles, expect improvement! It will come.

On warmer days, we would go outside. Any hard, flat surface is
okay: street (watch the cars), sidewalk, driveway. It's not necessary
to have a basket to practice dribbling! I would always have my son
or daughter start by dribbling, back and forth, over a 50 foot distance, right hand one way, left hand coming back. It helps, it works!

HOW TO DRIBBLE

Finger control. The ball is dribbled with the fingers, particularly the thumb and the three middle fingers. Some kids initially
will use the palm of the hand. However, the palm has only a limited
role in helping the fingers to receive and cradle the ball.The fingers
do most of the work. We want the ball out on the fingers and the
upper palm near the fingers as much as possible.

(See Figure 2.) The upper palm and lower thumb area are often needed to receive the bounced ball, especially if you are on the run, but then the fingertips take over. They direct the downward dribble as the ball rolls off the fingertips.

Receive, Cradle, and Pump. When little kids start dribbling for the first time, their natural impulse is to *strike* the ball downward when dribbling. The hand should not strike the ball, rather it reaches for and *receives* it well before the top of its bounce, *cradles* it for a split second, and then *pumps* it back to the floor. The hand actually *withdraws* as it meets the ball, so that it catches the ball, controls it, and then directs it down again. The idea here is to maximize the amount of time the hand is in contact with the ball, and this allows for greater control. Often in dribbling the player needs to make sudden moves or change speeds. Therefore, the hand needs to have sufficient contact and control so that these moves can be made. It helps to be able to send the ball back out in the direction desired with appropriate velocity. (See Figure 3.)

The point of contact between the hand and the ball will vary, depending on the direction the player will take. Usually, the index and middle fingers are on top of the ball, with the fingertips at or just forward of the uppermost point of the ball's curve. However, if the player is running with the ball, the fingers make contact farther back from the top center so they can push the ball forward. If a left turn is needed, then the fingers will cradle the ball more from the right side. There used to be stricter rules against cradling the ball from underneath, called carrying or *palming*. This allows the palm and fingers to completely control direction. This is rarely called any more in the pros, unless the violation is flagrant. (See Figure 4.)

Move with Rhythm. In order to accomplish all of this, the entire arm and shoulder move in a pumping action, raising at the shoulder and bending at the elbow. The concept you want to get across to your child is one of *rhythm*. The arm pumps in rhythm with the ball's bouncing. This rhythm is the essence of dribbling.

Get your child to understand the rhythm between the pumping action of the arm and the ball's bouncing. Get him to think about that rhythm while practicing. During a game they won't have time to think about it, but if he practices regularly, it will become natural.

The next step then is to get the *entire body* moving in the same

Figure 3
RECEIVE, CRADLE, AND PUMP

Hand extends to reach for the ball

Fingertips receive it and begin to withdraw

Hand withdraws, cradling the ball at top of the bounce

Then pump it back down

Figure 4
FINGER POSITIONING ON A DEAD RUN

*On the run, the hand comes up
behind the ball . . .*

*. . . and the fingers rotate up to
pump it out and down*

rhythm, that is, we hook up the feet into the pumping of the arm
and the bouncing of the ball. The concept is the same. First, explain
that the entire body must move in the same rhythm. A good drill for
this is the stutter step. Have your child separate his legs, left foot
forward, and move forward with a small hopping or stutter step, in
rhythm with the ball. The left foot is always forward, but small steps
are taken, pushing off the back foot. This drill builds the sense of
rhythm so essential to good dribbling. I tell my kids to remember
the movie *Rocky III* when Apollo taught Rocky how to get rhythm.
He used a stutter step too! If your child practices in the cellar,
turnon a radio and have her dribble dance to the beat of the music.

Develop both hands. If a player can dribble with only one
hand, usually the right hand since most kids are righties, then their
ability to move will always be limited. Defenders usually cheat a bit
to cut off the space to the dribbler's right. The ability to then switch
to the left hand and drive to the left side, opens a whole new dimension and substantially improves a player's offensive potential.

You need to continually remind your child to use both hands. Don't nag, just encourage her to devote some time for the other hand.

If she is a righty, have her spend time using only the left hand. When you apply pressure to her right side, be sure she attempts the left-handed drive. It will be difficult, sloppy, and awkward for her at first, so be supportive. Remind her that she will improve, praise the first sign of improvement. Remind her how hard it seemed to learn to whistle or ride a bike at first, and how easy it was once she got the hang of it. (See Figure 5.)

Head up, Eyes front. A child initially dribbles with his head down, keeping the ball in his field of vision, for obvious reasons. As he improves and develops a feel for the ball and its rhythm, he will be able to direct his attention more to what's going on *around* him. To the extent he keeps his head down, then to that extent he is unaware of opportunities around him: Who is open for a pass, what lane is available for advancing the ball, which way is the defender leaning, what opportunities are developing from the flow of play?

Figure 5
USE LEFT HAND

*Here mom blocks the righty lane forcing the dribble
with the left hand, a great drill!*

I wouldn't harp on this too much. The head will come up as the player becomes experienced enough to know where the ball is by *feel* instead of by *sight*. You need to talk to your child about the concept and why it's helpful to be able to focus on the whole floor. There are drills which can help, such as closing the eyes in order to force more reliance on *feeling* the ball's motion. Patience is needed here since much practice is required before the feel of the ball is sufficiently developed. It is useful however to quietly remind your child, every once in a while, to try to lift his attention, to be more broadly aware of what's going on around him. (See Figure 6.)

Keep the ball low, the body balanced and relaxed. A high bouncing dribble is easy to steal. Also, the longer the ball is away from the hand, the fewer the opportunities to change direction or react quickly. During drills, remind your child to keep the ball low, keep the dribbling hand low, keep the dribbling elbow low, keep the center of gravity of the body low. Practice keeping the dribble at knee height. Have her observe and feel the differences between a high and low dribble. In a low dribble, the tempo and rhythm is much faster, the ball is more under control. (See Figure 7.)

Figure 6
KEEP EYES UP – DRIBBLE BY FEEL

*If the eyes are down, you can't
see what's around you*

Eyes up, and all options are open

Figure 7
DRIBBLE LOW

Low dribbles are hard to steal . . .   *. . . and are much easier to control*

The body should always feel balanced, graceful, weight forward on the balls of the feet. Staying in touch with the rhythm of the ball and staying relaxed will help greatly. The great players make it look effortless because they are balanced, relaxed, in touch with the ball, and confident in their ability.

Keep the body between the ball and the defender. This is also called shielding. The idea is that the defender can't get to the ball without fouling if the dribbler keeps his body between the defender and the ball. Again, this is more easily done if he can dribble with both hands. While the dribbling elbow is in close, the other elbow is out shielding the body (but don't push with it). (See Figure 8.)

PIVOTS, FAKES, AND FEINTS

Often a player will receive a pass on the run, so she can continue to use her momentum and speed to its best advantage. This is

Figure 8
SHIELD THE BALL WITH THE BODY

Defender on the right, then dribble lefty

Use shoulder to shield, but don't foul with it

the case for mid-court passes, for the final pass in a give and go play, and for other passes to a player cutting toward the basket. If there is a free lane in front of the player, then it's almost always best to move directly through it and advance the ball. However, more often a player will receive a pass while closely guarded. So this requires her to put a move on the defender, get the defender to lean or commit to one side, and then quickly dribble the other way while the defender is off balance. This is done by faking to one side and then going to the opposite side.

Before further discussing the specifics of faking, we need to understand the concept of the *pivot*. For some reason, kids tend to learn the concept slowly and this severely limits their range of opportunity. They feel that their feet can move only while dribbling. The pivot rule, however, allows a player to pivot freely on one foot. The toes of the pivot foot cannot leave the floor and cannot slide, but he can rotate on those toes as much as needed and the heel *may* leave the floor. A player closely guarded by a defender can pivot 180 degrees in order to get the defender behind him, thus protecting the ball. (See Figure 9.) A pivot can also be part of a fake, stepping sharply in one direction to get a defender off balance and then pivoting back to the other direction.

There are several types of fakes. Keep in mind that most fakes require that the player be able to dribble with both hands. Once a defender knows that you can dribble only to one side, then any fakes to the other side are not effective.

Body fake. A most common fake is a full body fake. Here, using the right foot as a pivot, the player steps sharply toward the left, bringing the body and ball to the left. He then pivots quickly back to the right, driving off the pivot foot. (See Figure 10.) The idea with all fakes is to get the defender to *believe* you will move one way so he follows you. I find it useful to teach the kids to think they are actually *pulling* the defender off balance, and then suddenly change direction. The direction change must be very quick in order to dart through the lane opened by the fake. Tell your child to drive right by the defender and aggressively step into and claim the lane,

Figure 9
THE PIVOT

Defender approaches, ball handler has established right foot as pivot

Ball handler pivots on right toes, counter clockwise to protect the ball

leaving only inches away from the defender. If the defender comes back, he will commit a foul.

Head, shoulder, or Ball fake. This is just a variation of the fuller fake. The idea is to fake the head, the shoulder, the ball, or any combination of these three, just to get the defender to hesitate and then very quickly snap back the other way. (See Figure 11.)

Double fake. The double fake includes a half-hearted fake one way, and a full intensive fake the other. If the defender tries to outsmart you, thinking he has picked up the first fake and goes the other way, head in the direction of the first fake. The idea is not so much to plan a series of fakes, but rather to feel the defender's balance and take advantage of the first mistake he makes.

Shot or pass Fake. This is probably the most effective fake in basketball. The player pretends to take a set or jump shot (but the pivot foot does *not* leave the ground) and then as the defender comes forward or jumps to defend the shot, simply dribbles around him. Young players fall for this often! It's important to look at the

Figure 10
FULL BODY FAKE

Step sharply to the left with whole body and ball

Then drive to the opposite side, close to the defender

Figure 11
HEAD AND BALL FAKES

Head and shoulder fake

Ball fake to the left

basket and really pretend to shoot to get the defender to come forward. Sometimes the player may only need to raise the ball quickly to get a defender to react. Similarly, a player may pretend to pass the ball to a teammate, hoping the defender will lean toward the pass, and then dribble the opposite way.

Feint. Another effective fake is to change speed while dribbling. The player can pretend to speed up with a big explosive step and then slow down suddenly. Often the defender will be caught off balance. Any change in speed while dribbling can be quite effective in unbalancing a defender.

DRILLS

We've touched on a number of drills already in this chapter. The main idea in dribbling is just to do it and keep doing it. In cold weather, practice in the basement on a concrete floor. Otherwise, go out to the driveway or sidewalk. Practice just fooling around with the ball, switching hands, sudden movements (behind the back, between the legs), and practice speed dribbling; use both hands, use two balls, close the eyes, practice fakes.

Parents should get involved by applying some pressure. Create an obstacle for your child to dribble around, reach out to steal the ball. Apply enough pressure to make it a challenge, but *don't dominate*. Win a few, lose a few. Make it fun!

Cone drill. Set up some cones in a line about 3-5 feet apart and have her dribble, weaving through the cones. When she gets to the end she speed dribbles back. Then start over again. Use a stopwatch or a watch with a second hand to measure the best time and then have her run against the clock. (See Figure 12.)

One−on−One. The best drill is to let your child start at the top of the key. Have her put a fake on you as you defend, and then drive toward the basket for a layup.

Keep−Away. Two players stay inside a 10 foot square. One dribbles, one tries to get the ball. This drill teaches how to use the body to shield the ball.

King of the Hill. Several players dribble in a square area and try to tap each other's ball away, outside the square, with one hand, while dribbling with the other. The last one "alive" wins.

Figure 12
CONE DRIBBLING

This is a great drill. Use about six cones, even plastic cups will do

2.

PASSING

THE NATURE OF PASSING

Nothing is more important to team play than good passing. Your child will play less if he or she tends to throw the ball away, so they must learn the importance of snappy pass work. A bad pass causes the receiver to break or lose momentum and usually results in a lost opportunity or a turnover, losing the ball to the opponent.

A good pass can set up an easy shot. As stated in the prior chapter, kids often just want to go out and shoot, shoot, shoot. I have no problem with shooting, just put it in perspective and make sure other skills are also developed. The point about good dribbling and good passing is that they *lead* to good shots. The great ball players, Bob Cousy, Magic Johnson, Larry Bird, are better known for their incredible passing ability than for shooting. As I look back at my own playing days (I was tall and always played under the hoop), the times I scored a lot occurred when the team had a really good passing guard. His passes gave me easy shots underneath, so he made me look good.

Unfortunately, passing is the nemesis of youth basketball. It is a *team* skill, so it requires "two to tango." If either the passer or the receiver makes a mistake, the ball can easily be lost to the opposing team. At the very young ages, the passing is quite bad and confusion reigns. In most clinics, players are not allowed to press; that is, they must allow the opposing team to move the ball past the mid-court line before they can defend or try to steal. Were it not for

PITKIN COUNTY LIBRARY
120 NORTH MILL
ASPEN, CO 81611

such a rule, the kids would rarely get the ball very far up court.

Actually, the biggest problem with passing at young ages is just inexperience and the lack of confidence that comes from inexperience. A kid gets the ball and just freezes. He feels awkward and clumsy. Opposing players take advantage of the hesitation and close in on him. He does not know how to dribble out of it. He panics a bit and *closes off his awareness of where his teammates are* so he doesn't see them for a pass. Often, the player will just pivot, turn his back to the defender, and cover up! As a result, he either has the ball stolen from his hands or has a jump ball called because an opponent gets a hand on the ball. If he is closely guarded and holds the ball for over five seconds, he loses the ball on a five second violation. Another result may be that he just makes a bad pass. Chances are you will see your child in this situation. If you do, relax, it is common. It comes because he or she has not played enough. Make sure you tell your child this, and resolve to work a bit harder to improve basic skills.

There is no quick cure to this problem. Practice with dribbling will allow the player to dribble out of jams and allow her to keep her head up and open her focus or attention to the *whole floor*, as stated in Chapter 1. Once a player has stopped dribbling, the pivot moves will very effectively protect the ball and buy time to spot an open teammate for a pass. The pivot should not be just a cover−up, however, and it is preferable to face the defender strongly, fake him, and dribble or pass around him. Also, the coach will teach the kids some plays in which players move according to prearranged patterns, the main idea of which is to get a player open for a pass and an easy shot. It helps to know ahead of time where teammates are *supposed* to be and thus to anticipate where the pass should go. finally, as players play together for a time, they begin to know each other's moves.

You need to be patient here. Good passing can only be developed with experience. It's important to teach your child to *look* for the open teammate. Ball-hogs don't last long in basketball. No matter how good they are, they are not good for the team if they won't pass. Teammates eventually retaliate and won't give the ball to a ball-hog. It always leads to trouble. If your child gets this way, you must try to help change his approach. It's not enough that he is better than the other kids, if that is indeed true. You must help him understand that only team players survive the long run.

On the other hand, there are some kids who always pass. They don't try to dribble; they never try to shoot. They just *don't want the ball*! If your child falls into this pattern, don't be alarmed. Many kids do. However, you need to build up their confidence. Words are helpful, but they are empty unless he or she regularly practices ball handling skills. There is no quick fix! But regular practice will definitely result in improvement. *You need to believe this if your child is to believe it*. I live right next to an outdoor basketball court, and over the years I have seen various children from the neighborhood on the court. The ones who show up most often improve and become decent ball players. Pretty soon, they are varsity high school players. It's as simple as that! Practice and repetition work. One need not "be born with it," it definitely can be learned. It's like learning how to type. It seems impossible at first, but with practice and experience it becomes second nature. It can be learned. So can basketball skills!

PASSING TECHNIQUES

So, when it comes to passing, it's setting up a good pass that's the key. Good passing is less a technical skill and more the result of good individual or team dynamics. There are, however, some basic techniques for passing and receiving the ball.

Use two hands. A basketball is pretty big; it's tough to control with only one hand. The activity on the court is fast and furious with many sudden movements. Nearly all short or mid-range passes are two-handed, and the main reason for this is to control the ball as it is passed. A one-handed pass can roll off the hand as it is thrown. Control it with two hands.

A more important reason we use two hands is because passes must happen very quickly. The ball is usually already in front of the body, and there is no time to wind up for a one-handed pass. The ball is passed from the front of the torso, and the second hand is needed to give strength and power to the pass.

Obviously, a full-court pass needs the full power of an extended arm and must be thrown like a baseball. Otherwise, we use both hands.

Spread fingers and rotate fingertips up and into chest area.
Holding the ball at its sides, the thumb and index finger are spread,
forming an oval with each other. The other fingers are spread at a
relaxed distance from each other, not too far. This hand position
maximizes both control of the ball and power coming through the
fingers. (See Figure 13.)

When a ball is caught or taken up from the dribbling position
the hands are on the side, fingers out, thumbs up, and the ball is
usually waist high. The passing motion begins by bringing the hands
up and back to the chest. The fingers rotate upwards and a bit back
toward the upper chest as far as is comfortable. When the hands rotate, the elbows lift a bit to get more shoulder strength into the ball.
The farther the hands rotate, the more power can be placed on the
ball as the fingers snap or whip outward.

The ball is passed from in close to the chest for maximum
power. Actually, the chest also moves forward and down as the
player steps toward the target.

Step toward the target. This helps both accuracy and power,
getting the body moving with the pass. However, it must be a *very
quick* step because the step will signal the pass and alert the defense
to try to steal. The concept is to add power and accuracy by moving
toward the target as much as possible. (See Figure 14.)

**Drive body and hands forward and snap the wrists and fin-
gers outward.** This is all one movement. Drive the ball directly outward in a straight line. Power is transmitted to the pass from the
whipping action of the wrists as the ball rolls off the fingers, princi-
pally the index finger, next to the thumb. The index finger is the
center of the pass, and is the last finger to touch the ball. Stay off
the heels of the feet.

Have your child think of these things as you have a catch or as
she passes the ball off a wall. (I used to use my cellar wall.) Have
her just think about her hand position as she catches the ball and
then passes it. Have her notice how far back she rotates the hands,
and how more power comes with a greater rotation. Have her notice how much more accuracy she gets from stepping toward the
target, and the power she gets from driving with the back leg. Tell
her to bend forward at the waist for even more power. *If she gets the
idea of the various building blocks of passing, she will naturally begin
to use them.* Your job is to make her aware of them and to help her

Figure 13
TWO HAND CHEST PASS

Thumb and index fingers form an oval

Rotate ball and fingertips up and into chest area, in close for power

Drive ball straight out in a whipping action, as the ball rolls off the fingers

Flick the wrists outward

Figure 14
STEP INTO THE TARGET

A strong quick step will add power and control

practice them. Even if your child is an advanced player, there is no more useful practice than a review of basics and mechanics.

THE DYNAMICS OF PASSING

Now that we have the mechanics of chest passing covered, let's talk a bit about other aspects of the successful pass.

Don't broadcast the pass. Good defenders already have a knack for anticipating when to intercept passes. The worst thing to do is look right at the target before a pass. You might as well just pass it right to the defender. The defender already knows his man is open for a pass, he just doesn't know when it's coming, so we don't tell him by looking right at the target.

After playing a while, it doesn't take long, players develop what is called *floor vision*. They can see what's going on in front of them without having to focus on any one player. So they can *see* an open teammate without really looking at him. Since they never focus directly on the receiver, the defensive player is not tipped off.

Sometimes, a good passer sees his target and then looks at another player while passing to the first target. This ability is quite valuable since it gets defenders off balance.

Lead the receiver, use his momentum. If a player is cutting toward the basket, we don't want to slow him down by passing behind him. If you pass directly at him, by the time the ball arrives he will already be past it. So the passer must pass to where the receiver will be, slightly in front of where the receiver is at the time. Judge the speed of the receiver and pass the ball to meet him. (See Figure 15.)

Hit in the chest. This is not a hard and fast rule. You actually want to get the ball to the receiver's hands. However, it's usually easiest to catch a ball about chest high, and players are supposed to keep their hands up anyway, so in front of the chest is where the hands should be. Obviously, don't throw at their head if the hands are at the waist! If the hands are down, a bounce pass is good. If a receiver is under the hoop, a high pass is more effective, since the player does not need to spend time bringing the ball up. Where the ball needs to be thrown varies, but chest high is the best rule of thumb. (See Figure 16.)

Throw away from the defender. If a defender is on the left side of your target, then that's *not* where we want to pass the ball. Pass it to the other side so she can use her body to shield the ball. Often the receiver will have a hand up to where she wants the ball, and that's the target. (See Figure 16.)

Bounce passes. These passes are good in close situations, when the traffic is heavy. The bounce pass helps to get the ball down under the defender's hands. One problem with the bounce pass is that the floor slows the ball down. Also, this pass will need to be caught fairly low, which is not usually desirable. So it should be used only when needed to get the ball under and past a defender.

Overhead and baseball pass. The overhead pass is used to get a pass over the head of a defender. It's seen often to the outlet after a rebound. The ball is held high over the head and the arms are fully extended. The body is snapped forward at the waist, and the shoulders snap forward as well. The baseball pass is a one-handed throw, like throwing a baseball. It's used primarily for very long passes, usually as part of a fast break or to break a press. At young ages, it is not used often since it's rather hard to catch, and also

Figure 15
LEAD THE RECEIVER

Pass so they receive the ball out in front, running

Figure 16
CHEST HIGH PASS – AWAY FROM DEFENDER

The easiest pass to catch is chest high

Throw ball away from the defender, hit the target

Figure 17
OVERHEAD AND BASEBALL PASS

Arms extended overhead, snap ball to the target

For very long passes, just throw it like a baseball

since the rules usually do not allow fast breaks. (See Figure 17.)

Fake-shot pass. One of the more effective passes in basketball follows a fake jump shot. Just as the player is poised at the top of his jump, ready to shoot, he passes off to a teammate underneath. The defenders are caught off balance, expecting the shot and beginning to jockey for a possible rebound. The fake-shot pass serves to ensure that the ball gets to the receiver untouched, since defenders don't expect it, and it buys the receiver some time to get the shot off. The only problem is that sometimes you fake out your own man, and he misses the pass too! But that's his problem; he must always be alert and ready to receive the ball.

RECEIVING THE PASS

Know where the ball is and want it. The art of passing is mainly in the pass itself. Receiving the pass is not complicated. However, *many* passes are not caught or are bobbled. The most important skill in receiving the pass is simply being alert. Herein lies the greatest difference between the decent and the poor ball player. *You must always expect the ball!* Look at any youth basketball game and you will see that some kids get a lot of loose balls and rebounds and others don't. Some kids seem never to be looking when the ball is passed to them. Some kids never have the ball passed to them because they are not looking for it; they don't make eye contact with the passer. They don't seem to want the ball.

Players should never turn their backs to the ball, unless it's part of a play. They must always *know where the ball is*, and keep it in their field of vision. Most important, they should always be prepared to receive a pass, always be looking for the ball — *they've got to want the ball*. This is the key!

Kids who *want* the ball are easy to pick out. They play more aggressively. They are constantly trying to get into position for a pass. Their eyes are on the passer, searching to see if she will pass the ball, signalling they are ready for it with a hand up as a target. They dive for loose balls.

Some of this quality seems inborn, but it can be developed. It grows with confidence. Tell your child that he must *always want* the ball. Part of the problem, where there is a problem, comes from lack of confidence. Some kids don't want the ball because they are afraid they will make a mistake. They somehow manage never to be open for a pass. Deal with this by practicing! As skills improve, so does confidence. If you play one-on-one with your child, he will learn what he can do with the ball. He will learn that he can handle the ball, and he will want the ball more often.

Move to the ball. Unless the pass is part of a play, like a give and go, the receiver must reach for, and if possible step to, the ball. Defenders will look to steal the pass, so it's important to beat them to it. Many, many passes are stolen because the receiver was flat-footed, waiting for the ball. Step to it, and reach out the hands to receive it! Claim the ball! (See Figure 18.)

Give a target. It's much easier on the passer if the receiver puts up a hand, palms out, to the spot they want the ball. For instance, if a defender is on the right side, put up a left hand as the target.

Hands must be soft. A basketball is big and very bouncy, so it's rather difficult to catch. Many kids tense up when the ball approaches, and this increases the chance that the ball will bounce off

Figure 18
MOVE TO THE BALL

*The most important thing in receiving is to move or
step to the ball*

their hands.

Tell your child that she must try to be relaxed. Shake her hands, loosen them up. Make them less tense and rigid. *Soft hands* is a term used in all sports: baseball, football. In soccer, we talk of soft feet. Practice passing and receiving with your child and discuss this concept. Tell her to notice her hands, to make them soft, and then to notice the difference.

Keep the eyes on the ball. This is the key to catching anything in any sport. The ball is pretty big, and easy to see, but that does not lessen the need to concentrate on it. Watch the ball from the moment it leaves the passer's hands until it's in your hands. Maintain concentration. It's okay to divide concentration, to begin to sense what to do with the ball, but never take the eyes from it. The transition from the catch to the next movement, whether it is a dribble, pass, or shot, requires *control* of the ball. Control begins with a solid reception.

PASSING DRILLS

We already discussed the best passing drill there is. You and your child just go out and have a catch. You don't need a basket, and this can be done anywhere, even in your cellar. I used to do it all the time with my sons (just clear away breakables!). Passing off a concrete wall is useful for someone who is practicing alone.

Talk about the importance of passing as you and your child have a catch. Talk about the techniques, finger positions, rotation, stepping to the target. Talk about dynamics. Talk about receiving with soft hands, keeping the eye on the ball, moving to the ball, weight forward. I used to stand about 5 feet from my son and we would pass the ball quickly back and forth, as quickly as we could, almost tipping it back and forth. This drill forces you to concentrate on the ball, and develops quicker reflexes.

Monkey-in-the-middle. This is a good drill because it teaches dribbling, passing, and receiving with some pressure. Three players are needed. Set up a 12 foot square, put markers at the corner (any flat hard surface will do). The "monkey" tries to intercept or force a turnover. Whoever makes the mistake (five seconds delay, bad pass, a missed reception, traveling) is the new monkey. Make sure the kids use the pivot move a lot. Watch the fouls, don't let the monkey reach in and foul.

Keep away. This drill is like monkey-in-the-middle, but here it's two on two. We covered this drill in Chapter 1; however, here we change it a bit. Only left-handed dribbling is allowed. There are many variations depending on what skill you wish to emphasize. The point is that it's a good drill for teaching multiple skills.

On the run. Two players start at one end of a court, or on your sidewalk or driveway, and run to the other end, passing back and forth. Try it with and without dribbling. Watch the traveling fouls: only one step is allowed before a dribble is required.

Weaving. Three players go the length of the court; the player who passes then runs toward and behind the receiver. (See Figure 19.)

Figure 19
THE WEAVE DRILL

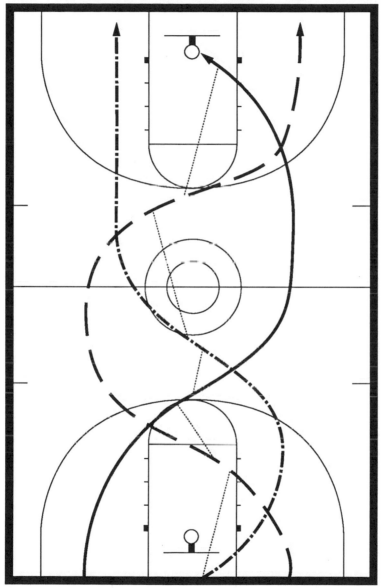

Three solid or broken lines represent the players.
Passes are the small dotted lines. Each player passes
the ball to the player in front of him and then cuts
behind that player, sprinting up court to receive a pass
from the third player, and so on

3.

SHOOTING

THE SHOOTERS

Shooting is fun, it's the essence of basketball. I'll never forget the smiles that broke across the faces of kids as they made their first basket ever in a game.

A kid who can *consistently* hit shots is a rare and valuable player. Teams often build their offense around their best shooter, running plays that will get this player free for a good shot. *It is not essential* that your child be a good shooter, but if she can't shoot, she will need to be very good at dribbling and passing or rebounding. Role players are important. Most kids will not become great shooters, and that is why it's so important to develop other skills.

There are *outside shooters* and *inside shooters*. An outside shooter is someone who can sink about half of his shots from 12 feet or farther. They are the chosen people of basketball. A winning team almost always must have a good outside shooter. I played in a youth league as a kid and we had a great shooter named Rich. He scored twenty points a game and led us to a championship. It was great to know he was on the court, and could stick the ball when things got close!

Everyone on the team must be a decent inside shooter. Tall players will obviously be called upon to do most of it, but everyone needs to be able to deliver two points most of the time when shooting underneath. It's a different kind of shot, mainly *banking* the ball off the backboard or soft-touching it gently over the rim. It takes a sense of touch, knowing how hard to hit the ball against the backboard. At young ages the kids usually bank it way too hard and the ball bounces away off the rim.

The good news for parents is that shooting can be learned, so it can also be taught. Sure, naturally talented kids will learn a lot faster, but *all kids* can learn to shoot. It takes thousands of shots to raise a shooter's percentage, but it really doesn't take that long to shoot a thousand shots!

In 1989, I had an experience with my older son, Jack, which was the most memorable coaching experience of my life. I think it's the best testimony to what an individual parent can do, and it may be the best information I can leave you with in this book.

My son was entering his junior year in high school. He had played basketball, but for a number of reasons, including injuries, he had not gotten a lot of playing time or experience. He was tall and quick, and very much wanted to be able to contribute more during his final two high school years. He and I discussed it, and we agreed that we would spend the summer in an intensive program. I would coach him, so we spent hours, every day during the summer, working on skills. I would stand under the hoop and rapidly feed him rebounds for short jump shots. He shot and shot until his arms nearly fell off. He would dribble, shoot fouls, and play one-on-one against me. By the time we were done, he couldn't miss short jump shots. His coach told me he had never seen such improvement, and Jack eventually broke into the starting lineup. This is a boy who was cut as a freshman! This experience taught me how much difference a parent can make in helping a child to improve, especially when the child is motivated. Parents can make a difference!

You need to be patient with your child at young ages. Kids develop shots at differing paces. It will come with practice. I coached a clinic for eight and nine year olds a few years ago. One boy, named Eric, was one of the most talented athletes in the group. He was so full of energy that he could *not* make a basket. He just banged the ball off the backboard. A few years later, when Eric was twelve, I saw him play on my son's school team. He was still rough,but you could see the beginnings of gracefulness. The boy will be a great player some day, but for many kids it just takes time and perseverance. Perhaps the greatest contribution a parent can make is to help the child get past the frustrating experience of being a beginner. Help your child hang in there!

OUTSIDE SHOOTING – MECHANICS AND DYNAMICS

The introduction of the three point play, a long shot of over 19 feet, has restored outside shooting to basketball at the college level. At youth levels, most kids can't shoot that far. However, it brings a needed dimension back to the game, and gives shorter players a chance to develop a skill which will give them more playing time.

Kids know who can shoot the ball. Coaches know too. If a kid can shoot he's told to go for it. If a kid can't consistently make a certain shot, he's told just that! If you can't do it, don't waste the shot. It has nothing to do with personalities, at least it shouldn't. If you have it, use it, otherwise only do what you can do. It makes sense. In practice, the kids are given a chance to show what they have. However, an outside shot is not developed during team practice. A player must do that on his own time. It takes 10,000 shots. My younger son plays with a boy named Matt, who spends hours nearly every day, even in the rain, shooting jump shots in his driveway. The boy can shoot, so he will always be allowed to take the outside shot. It's a privilege which must be earned. He earned it by shooting tens of thousands of shots. This is not to say that other players can't shoot from the outside from time to time, but it is in the team's best interest for kids to do what they do well, and most of the time that's what they should do. They should shoot from a distance at which they can make a shot over half the time.

We'll cover offensive play-making in Chapter 6. Suffice it to say that a play is a series of movements designed to free up a shooter, usually by screening or picking off the player who is defending him. If the play works, a shooter is open to take a high percentage shot. High percentage shots are mainly shots within the player's range, which are taken with a minimum of defensive pressure, thus allowing the shooter to use good shooting form.

Let's discuss the mechanics of outside shooting.

The stance: Feet balanced, triple threat. We'll cover the *triple* *threat* stance in the chapter on offensive dynamics. It basically is a position from which the player can execute a shot, a dribble, or a pass, in any direction, including fakes. The weight is forward on the balls of the feet. The feet are balanced under the shoulders and pointed toward the basket. The knees and waist are bent, ready to move in any direction, head and *shoulders are square and level*, head and chin are up, the ball is up in front of the chest, elbows are out to protect it. (See Figure 20.)

Fake a pass or jab step to ground the defender. Often the play-making will get the ball to an open player who just quickly shoots the ball. However, if defended, the player will need to get the defender off balance so she can't block the shot. Usually, a faked dribble or *jab step* will get a young defender to move to the side or back up, thus allowing an unobstructed shot. As soon as the player gets the ball she steps strongly toward, right at, the defender. Then, when the defender reacts and takes a step back, the shooter takes an unobstructed shot. (See Figure 21.)

Figure 20
TRIPLE THREAT STANCE

*Weight forward on feet, knees and waist bent, head
up, shoulders square, ball up by chest*

Figure 21
JAB STEP AND SHOOT

Jab step right at the defender, who then also steps backward

Then snap back and shoot

You can't overemphasize the importance of fakes. If a player gets a hand up in the shooter's face, the shooting percentage drops considerably. The best way to communicate this concept is to tell your child to try to *feel the defender's balance.* The player tries to mentally *push* the defender off balance into one direction or the other, and can almost *feel* them leaning one way or the other. Also, trying to *relate* to the defender's balance helps to make the fake convincing. The defender must believe that the shooter is going to dribble. This can be practiced. Have your child try to fake you, and then you try it while he is defending.

Jump high, straight up, off both feet. The highest percentage jump shot is straight up. Players sometimes get in the habit of leaning to one side as they jump and this will result in a slight ball motion to that direction. Sure, sometimes defensive pressure will *force* a shooter to lean, or fade away (lean backwards). Sometimes (not often) a player can even perfect such a shot. But the higher percentage is always straight up, thus ensuring that the shooter

Figure 22
JUMP STRAIGHT UP

*Straight up is the highest percentage shot,
don't lean*

does not have to calculate and compensate for body lean. (See Figure 22.) Also, a straight jump will get the ball higher, over the tips of the defender's fingers. The whole idea of the *jump shot* is just that, to reduce the odds that the shot will be blocked. So teach your child to jump high, get both feet involved, springing off the toes. Practice this. We want the jump high, but we also want it graceful. The idea is to jump as high as is comfortable. The ball is released just before the peak of the jump, as the player enters the peak. This gets the legs into the shot. *Remember to tell your child that a shot starts in the legs.* Talk about the lazy jump shot. It can be more easily blocked, and the shot itself is less accurate, less intense. Moreover, using both feet adds to the balance and control of the jump, thus improving the odds for a goal.

Cradle the ball high, shoulders square, point shooting, elbow toward the hoop. The most important technique in outside shooting is the position of the shooting elbow. It must aim toward the basket.

Figure 23
CRADLE HIGH – SHOULDERS SQUARE – POINT ELBOW

With elbow pointed outward the shot is much tougher

Here elbow is pointed straight, hand cradled high, and shoulders squared

Often kids point that elbow outward a bit, and *this must be changed.* Keep the elbow in. More than anything else, more than a body lean, an outward elbow will send a ball in an errant direction. It will prevent the wrist from properly launching the ball. The upper shooting arm should be, generally, parallel to the floor, and it must always point in the *direction* of the basket. (See Figure 23.)

The hands form a *cradle* for the ball, the shooting hand a bit lower and more behind the ball, and the non-shooting hand straight up on the opposite side. The concept of the cradle is important because we want to control the ball but not squeeze it. The hands gently cradle the ball as if it were sitting on a launching pad, and then the wrist flicks it out. Only one hand shoots, the other is passive and simply falls away. Kids *often* shoot with two hands, since they are not strong enough to shoot with one. However, they must understand that one-handed shots are higher percentage shots.

Figure 24
CRADLE THE BALL HIGH

The cradle is a launch pad, shooting hand under, guide hand aside

Rear view, keep the cradle high, kids tend to push from the chest, but it must be overhead

The cradle is held high, in front of and over the head. The eyes see the basket from *under* the ball, between the arms. Again, we hold the hands high to minimize the chances of a blocked shot. The cradle also needs to be high enough so we can see the hoop under the ball. The head and shoulders are level, square, so that the body is balanced, straight up. (See Figure 24.)

At the top of the jump, flick the wrist, placing a 30 degree spin on the ball with the thumb side of the hand. We shoot just before the top of the jump, again to avoid the defender's outstretched hands. We also want to ensure that some of the strength of the jump is transferred to the ball. A shot begins in the legs and the power is transferred to the ball.

The wrist flick is as important as pointing the elbow at the hoop. Most kids develop all kinds of crazy hand techniques, such as closing the fingers into a fist as they shoot, or coming down with the middle finger or little finger. The natural and correct form is to flick the ball out of the cradle by turning the palm *down and out*. The little finger stays in the same position, pointing upward, before and after the shot. The thumb, however, moves 180 degrees and finishes pointing downward and similarly with the index finger. It is the index finger which does most of the work of shooting.

When the shooting hand turns down and out, this serves to put a reverse 30 degree (from the vertical) spin on the ball. That's how you know it has been done properly. (See Figure 25.) The final hand position is called a *gooseneck*. The left hand does not add any power on a right-handed shot. It passively cradles the ball and then merely falls away. Many years ago, most shots were two-handed set shots, but it has long been understood that a one-handed shot is a higher percentage shot. The shooting hand does *not* snap back, but gently follows through the shot in a downward arc. It may also just be held relatively stationary for a moment. Either style is okay.

If your child does not properly flick the ball from the cradle, then he should modify his shot. It's always difficult, but it can be done with some drills, particularly if you catch it early enough. I feel the best way to change form is to shoot repeatedly against a high wall, and just go through a few hundred wrist flicks. A few such practice sessions will help to make any correction needed. Good form is essential in shooting.

Aim to set the ball on or just beyond the front of the hoop. Concentration is essential to good shooting. The idea is to reduce any unnecessary movement, be balanced and still. Focus the eyes on the point of the hoop closest to the shooter and try to set the ball on top of that spot. This *reduces the focus to a single point*, instead of the whole space of the hoop. The shooter tries to loft the ball and set it down just on or past the point of the hoop closest to him.

Try to get a reasonable *arc* to the ball path. A lot of players shoot *bricks*, a term used to define a ball that travels directly *at* the basket. However, the ball needs to *drop* through the hoop, and a linear shot has a smaller window through the hoop than a shot with an arc. Obviously, a linear shot is straighter, since it is one dimensional, but it also has less chance of scoring. On the other hand, a *very* high arc is unnecessary, and it also lowers the percentage. For a comfortable arc, a rule of thumb is to peak the arc at about 3-4 feet

Figure 25
THE GOOSENECK
FLICK THE WRIST

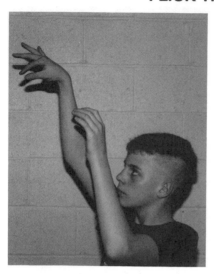

Let the left hand fall away, and flick the ball from the cradle

The final hand posture should look like this gooseneck

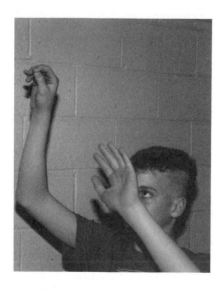

Some kids squeeze their fingers like this, not allowing the wrist full play

Others will shoot with the middle two fingers, again not allowing full wrist action

Figure 26
ARC THE SHOT

Here the ball arcs about four feet above the hoop on a
15 foot shot

higher than the basket on a 15 foot shot. (See Figure 26.) In close, a
1 to 2 foot arc is okay.

Follow the shot. I think the toughest habit for a kid to break is
that of watching the ball as it moves to the basket. A small but sig
nificant percentage of rebounds bounce back toward the shooter,
and a player who follows the shot toward the basket will often get a
rebound and a second chance, a good number of times. When you
practice shooting with your son or daughter, tell them always to
take at least one or two steps forward following the shot, just to develop the habit. The habit of standing there watching the ball is
usually developed during shooting practice, and it's a bad one.
Come down moving to the hoop. In fact, it's good to land a bit in
front of the take-off spot, leaning forward a *tiny* bit. We essentially
want the jump straight up, with a slight forward tilt.

Okay. That's the mechanics. We've already covered some dynamics of outside shooting, such as taking the high percentage shot
and getting the defender off balance. There are a number of other
dynamics to think about.

Always look first for the open man underneath. An outside shooter may be good, but she'll never shoot more accurately than a player underneath the hoop. Also, remember that a fake shot is a great decoy and a good opportunity to dump off to the big men underneath. A good team player is always looking for an open player with a better shot. That's how ball games are won — good percentage shooting.

Keep all options open. When faking, the idea isn't really to fake a dribble in order to shoot, or fake a shot in order to dribble, it's to do what the situation calls for. If the player takes the fake dribble, *then shoot*. Sometimes, you have to try several fakes and then capitalize on the one that works best. We discussed earlier the concept of feeling or relating to the defender's balance. Once she is off balance, then go the other way.

Adjust the shot if needed. Sometimes, many times, the defender will recover and get a hand up in front of the shooter. Then the shooter must react or she will eat the ball. Often it's enough to give the ball a bit more arc, enough to get over the hand or perhaps to go for a bank shot, which both adds arc and slightly changes direction. Another is to double pump, that is, to withdraw the hand momentarily and restart the shot. Alternately, the player can fade away from the defender, and lean back to get more shooting angle and arc. React to the defender, relate to the defender, sense where he or she is at all times and take what opportunities are given.

A common error in shooting is to shoot the ball too far, past the rim. If this happens, then chances are the forearm is too involved in pushing the ball. We need more wrist and less forearm.

Know your range and shoot with confidence. I'm not being negative when I say "know your range," but basketball *is* a team game. If your child hasn't spent the hours needed to shoot 15-19 foot shots, then don't practice them during a game. There is no individual right to shoot long shots. Most players can and should ordinarily take shots of 10 feet or less, if they can get the shot off without being blocked, but only players who earn the long ones should ordinarily take them. A player knows from practice what his or her range is. There is usually a range where they make most of the shots. Then there is a gray area, usually 10-15 feet. Finally, there is a range where they miss most shots. *Players should always take open shots they can hit over half of the time or better in practice.*

When a player is within his effective range, he should take a good shot fearlessly whenever he can. How often do we see a player refuse to take a simple 8 foot jumper because he is not confident? Shoot those shots, even poor shooters will make a lot of the shorter shots.

Of course, the best remedy for lack of confidence is simply more practice. That's where parents come in. The coaches need to use practice time for general dynamics and conditioning. Shooting practice gets little time. The coach will tell the kids how to shoot, but they expect the kids to practice shots on their own. The kids who do so will get more playing time, because they will put numbers up on the scoreboard. Coaches keep statistics, such as number of points, rebounds, steals, assists, turnovers — they all count! The kids with the numbers will play. Some coaches don't know talent if they fall over it, but the numbers usually don't lie, and that's how lineups are often made, based on the numbers.

INSIDE SHOOTING – MECHANICS AND DYNAMICS

Basketball is still a tall person's game. The highest percentage shooting, 70% or better, comes inside, underneath the hoop, or within 6 feet or so. It's the boiler room area of the court, where you'll find a lot of grunting, leaning, boxing-out, shot blocking, re-bounding, fancy lay-ups, slam dunks, hook shots, and soft-touch jumpers, sometimes banked off the glass. It's the world of basket-ball at its best. Sure, the three point shots have opened the game up, and a player with quick hands is valuable dribbling and stealing passes, but the game is still most exciting *in the paint*, the area be-tween the foul lines (usually painted in a different color). (See Figure 27.)

It's rare for a player to be successful underneath without at least average or above average height. Short players who are very quick can sometimes drive past the big men and get a shot off if they are agile. However, they can only visit but not live there. Big players get rebounds, block shots, and score points underneath. If your child is short, it's not a problem, but he must learn to

Figure 27
ACTION UNDERNEATH

Action in the paint

dribble, pass, and shoot outside. Guide him in the direction appropriate to his size.

There are basically three inside shots: the driving lay-up, the short jump shot, and the hook.

The lay-up. One of the themes I've taken in this book is confidence building, and it reflects my general approach to coaching. I believe it's good to get kids going, focus on *something they can use right away*, sort of jump-start the engine. Once a kid gets to a point that she can contribute to a team, confidence takes over and she will blossom like the yellow forsythia on the first warm spring day. Kids on a team will pass the ball to your child if they feel he or she can do something with it, otherwise they will tend to look for someone who can. This is why I emphasize dribbling so much. It's a skill that most quickly will get your child into a position from which confidence and all other skills will grow. I've seen it work countless times.

The same is true for lay-ups. At young ages, beginners, the scores are low. The players generally can't shoot outside (or inside).

A kid who can drive a few steps to the hoop and shoot a lay-up will have the best chance of scoring in youth basketball. Teach your son or daughter to do lay-ups and, more quickly than with any other skill, their confidence will grow and with it the ball player within them will emerge.

A lay-up is still the most exciting shot in basketball, and it's also one of the simplest. Kids dream of Michael Jordan dribbling toward the basket, leaping and flying through the air, and spinning into a reverse slam dunk. My thirteen year old son breaks into this imaginary move in our hallway every so often! Well, your child won't dunk for a while, but a drive and lay-up are certainly possible, and should be emphasized and perfected above all other forms of shooting.

The reason is simple. Outside shooting is tough. A kid has to shoot a few thousand shots before he or she can consistently hit the hoop. No problem, it just takes time. However, lay-ups can be learned more quickly. Also kids usually play pretty poorly on defense, so a player who can dribble a bit will be able to advance the ball up close for an inside shot. It looks good, and it will get a cheer from the fans. It will help the team, and your child will take a big step forward in development. Most important, it's easy to do and comes quickly with a little practice. Here are the basics:

1. *Make a move.* A lay-up usually starts when the player gets the ball about 10-15 feet from the basket. If it's a play, then the player just receives the ball on the run and continues to the hoop. Most often, however, a player gets a pass or rebound and needs to *make a move,* the basketball term for faking the defender. We have talked about fakes before, so I won't repeat it all here. The idea is to get the defender off balance, moving one way, and then drive (dribble) around him going the opposite way.

2. *Claim the lane and explode through it.* Once a lane for dribbling is available, the player very quickly claims it. We can't dribble through a stationary defender, but we can claim any open lane. I always say to drive as close to the defender as possible. If he reacts and moves back into that lane, *he will commit a foul.* The official will usually call the foul on a moving defender. Talk to your child about claiming the lane and sticking to it. It always helps to get the other team to foul. The idea is to pick a point just on the outside the defender's shoulder and drive your shoulder right by it. If the

defender reaches in, she fouls. Otherwise, break to the hoop!

3. *Submarine*. Keep everything low early in a driving lay-up — shoulders down, elbows in, waist and knees bent, head up, ball dribbled low to the floor. This helps quickness, increases ball control, and protects the ball. Don't bump the opponent, or lower the shoulder *into* him. Stay low and steady.

4. *Take the two free giant steps and find an opening.* The last two steps are the most important. They are free, that is, no dribble is required. (Actually, the first step comes off the last dribble and establishes the pivot, only one "free" step is technically allowed.) The player usually takes two giant steps to cover a fair bit of ground. Since he is no longer dribbling, he also has the opportunity to look up for an opening. The ball is held firmly in both hands and the player "feels" the defense. Usually, a big player underneath the hoop will react once you drive by a defender, so everything must happen very quickly. The two giant steps are often enough to get to a spot where the ball can be laid-up to the basket. *A great drill* for making this point is to have your child start at the foul line and make a lay-up *with only one dribble*! It's easily done, and it teaches the player how much distance he can cover without much dribbling. After practicing a while, have him do it from farther out, with only one dribble.

The best angle to take is 45 degrees to the hoop. Obviously, there is often no choice. If there is, come in at this angle since it maximizes ball control and use of the backboard.

5. *Lift the knee closest to the shooting hand and push straight up with the opposite foot.* Kids often push off the wrong foot, and it's important right away to get the proper footwork. If the lay-up is right-handed, then the right arm needs to stretch up, and the whole right side should lift with it. Raising the right knee does this. The concept to teach your child is to *raise the whole right side* on right-handed shots (vice versa for lefty lay-ups). It comes after a few practice sessions. Note that this means the first free step for a righty lay-up is with the right foot. At the beginning of that step, the player grabs the ball with both hands and prepares to shoot, finally driving off the left foot. Lifting the right knee also adds to the height of the jump. Finally, the player needs to remember to *jump straight up*. This not only adds to the height of the jump, but it also slows down the forward movement of the body so the ball hits the

backboard a bit more softly. (See Figure 28.)

6. *Lay the ball up softly off the glass.* The hardest thing about shooting lay-ups is controlling the speed of the ball off the backboard. The overwhelming majority of lay-ups are shot off the backboard. Teach your child to use the backboard at a young age. However, the overwhelming majority of missed shots arise because the ball hits the backboard too hard. The body is usually moving forward with speed and momentum. Jumping straight up slows it a bit, but we still need to ensure that the ball is laid-up softly. The ball sits in the palm of the right hand, palm turned partially inward toward the shooter. It also can be done with the palm outward, like a jump shot, but it's much tougher to control the ball speed. The hand tries to withdraw a bit from the body speed to slow the ball. As a player becomes experienced, spin may be applied to compensate for odd angles.

The backboards are usually marked with a square, and the player lays the ball up against the lines of the square. With practice, the player will shoot automatically and not need to look for the square.

Then the body rotates or twists counterclockwise a bit to prepare for a controlled landing. This rotation should be coached, but don't confuse things too much in the early stages. Just tell your child to twist a bit in order to land on balance.

7. *Dish the ball off if needed.* We mentioned that once the ball handler successfully passes a defender, a big player underneath will react to defend him. If this happens, it means this defender has abandoned the man he was guarding, who should then be free. If so, continue with the lay-up, get that big defender to commit fully, and then dish (pass) the ball off to the open player. It works like a charm!

8. *Practice the lefty shot.* Be patient here since developing a lefty lay-up (for righties) is the toughest thing in basketball. Start slowly. Urge your child to try it a few times. It will feel very awkward, don't confuse him. It will come along slowly. Just reverse the footwork. On the left side of the basket, a lefty shot is more effective since it allows the body to be between the defender and the ball. That's why it's needed. Discuss this concept.

9. *Be fancy in practice.* Some coaches discourage kids from shooting trick or fancy off-balance lay-ups during practice, but I

Figure 28
SHOOTING LAY-UPS

Lift the whole right side, leg and arm, jump straight up, drive off left foot

Lay the ball up softly on the glass

After laying the ball up, rotate body for easier landing

Practice fancy moves, they are often needed underneath

always encourage it. In a game the defender usually doesn't allow a textbook shot, the shooter often needs to contort. Therefore, it should be practiced. Let the kid have fun with it. Use the hang time, the air time, to double pump, twist, and change angles.

The short jump shots and chippies. These are the shots that get blocked most often. They are shot in close to the hoop where the big players roam and they don't have the advantage of body motion which a lay-up provides.

The mechanics of short shots are similar to those of longer outside shots except that here you need to be much more concerned about the defender, so the shot needs to be carried out very quickly, with quick moves and quick release. (See Figure 29.)

Fakes are even more important in close to the hoop. The best fake is to raise the ball quickly as if to shoot, get the defender to jump, and then go up as she comes down. Sometimes, a few fake pumps with the ball are needed.

Often a short jump shot can effectively use the backboard. It's a bit tougher, but it provides a higher and off-line arc, and this is

Figure 29
SHORT SHOTS

Take the open shot quickly, before defenders regroup

Fake and then shoot as the defender is coming down

tougher to defend. Otherwise, remind your child to focus on the point of the rim closest to her and to arch the ball softly to that spot. Also, a dish off to an open player is very effective. Ordinarily, any shot within 4-5 feet of the hoop and to the side should use the backboard. Jumpers in front of the hoop go directly to the rim.

The hook-shot. This is pretty much a big player's shot. It is used underneath the hoop, usually on a pass from an outside player when the shooter's back is initially to the hoop. The technique is to turn sideways to the hoop. Fake a turn one way, usually with the head and shoulder, and then lean the other way, turning off the right foot (for a righty hook) and jumping with strength from the left foot (or hopping and jumping off both feet). If the defender is moving, lean into her. Bring the ball up the right side of the body, hold it tightly, and then raise it with the right hand, holding it away from the defender, protecting it with the left side of the body. Focus on the point of the hoop closest to you, look at it specifically, and then flick the ball over it softly. The key here is jumping aggressively and looking at the nearest point on the rim. A big player *must* develop a hook shot. It's tough to defend, and can be very accurate if practiced. Like all shots, it should be practiced every time you play. (See Figure 30.)

Practice drills. The best way to practice shooting is just to shoot! Get the mechanics working properly and then shoot thousands of shots. Kids won't get to practice shooting much at team practices, as I said, so they have to do it on their own. This is where the parent can be most helpful. He or she shoots and you get the rebound and feed the pass back for another shot. You can do many repetitions in a relatively short time. I did this for a summer oncewith my older son and, as I noted, his shot accuracy improved dramatically. The great shooters practiced for hours a day as kids. After a while, put a little pressure on him as he shoots and go back for the rebound. Have him fake and drive around you, applying enough pressure to make it challenging (but don't overwhelm him). Ultimately, a game of one-on-one is great practice. I used to play my son at nine years old, and I would not use my hands to defend his shots (my head was about as high as a kid's hand and supplied sufficient pressure). I also would not raise my hands above my head to rebound − it kept things more even.

Figure 30
HOOK SHOT

Underneath, a hook is an essential shot

Feeding passes for shots is the best practice there is. Keep saying things like *point the elbow, cradle, flick the wrist, soft hands, eye on the front of the rim* (the point of the rim closest to them), *head and shoulders square, shoot quick, release quick, jump higher, fake the dribble, follow up the shot, shoot with confidence, shoot from your legs, feel graceful.* After a while, you will be chasing far fewer rebounds! (See Figure 31.)

FOUL SHOTS

Foul shots certainly deserve special mention. It can be said that foul shooting wins or loses most close games, and this is so at all levels of play. At youth ages, good foul shooting is rare, but since scores are usually low, a foul shooter can win a game.

Players get two free shots if fouled in the act of shooting and the shot is missed. Two shots are also awarded for any intentional or flagrant foul. If fouled in any other manner, they get foul shots only if the other team has accumulated five personal fouls during

Figure 31
FEEDING REBOUNDS

Probably the most helpful and the easiest thing a
parent can do is just to feed the child rebounds.
Repetition is so very important to good shooting

the half. One foul shot is awarded, and a second bonus shot is awarded if the first shot scores. This is called a one-and-one.

In lining up for foul shots, two defenders get the position closest to the hoop, between the block and the first lane markers, on both sides of the lane. Then two teammates of the shooter, and so forth. Players may enter the foul lane after the ball leaves the shooter's hand, but the shooter can't enter the lane until the ball touches the rim or backboard.

Shooting foul shots is much like shooting jump shots, except the feet don't leave the ground. In the old days, players like the great Wilt Chamberlain used to shoot fouls underhanded with two hands. However, the highest percentage shots, as said before, are one-handed flicks out of a cradle. The ball is brought over the head, cradled, and shot with one hand. The shooting hand ends up in a gooseneck, just as with jump shots. The head and shoulders are square to the hoop. The shooting elbow points at the hoop.

Much of foul shooting comes from the legs. They must bend and extend into the shot. The body starts low and fully extends, *up on the toes*, and the player stays up on the toes while the ball is in flight. This is the key, to stay extended into the shot.

It's also important to point the front foot, usually the right foot for a righty shot, *at the hoop*. Don't let it turn in because that will retard full extension. The other foot can be back a comfortable distance. Remember, as with all shooting, shoot with the legs.

Foul shots should be practiced, at least a few, preferably a minimum of twenty-five, at the *end* of each practice session, while the player is tired. (See Figure 32.)

Figure 32
FOUL SHOOTING

Foul shooting wins or loses games, depending on whether the players seriously practice this skill

4.
RULES OF THE GAME

KNOW THE BASICS

Don't just skip over this chapter, it is an important one. I coached a clinic for eight year olds one year and was surprised to see how little the kids knew of the jargon, the language of basketball. Sure, they had nearly all heard of a slam dunk, but that was about it.

So before each practice, we sat around in a circle and I had a list of new words for them. Words like *key, foul, walk, free-throw, double dribble, three seconds, jumper,* and *lay-up.* There are dozens and dozens of words like this that are unique to basketball. I'd do about ten words at each practice and we'd talk about their meanings. I'd first ask if any of the kids could explain the words to me, to get a dialogue going, then quickly review last practice's words.

It's important for your child to be familiar with the basic rules and terms. Sure, eventually his coach may get around to this, but some kids get embarrassed when their ignorance is the basis for the day's lesson. You can minimize this by having your child read this section, or by going over it with her. You can just take a list of the words as I did and go over a few at a time.

Learning the terminology is just one more way to breed confidence. It removes some of the mystery, the fear of the unknown. It all helps to get to that point where confidence replaces self concern, where the child's perspective turns outward to the team instead of inward, worried about himself, how he looks, or whether he is doing okay.

THE HISTORY OF BASKETBALL

Kids have been bouncing, kicking, and throwing balls and round things for as long as there have been kids and round things. However, basketball seems to have a fairly definite point of invention.

In 1891, a YMCA gym teacher in Springfield, Massachusetts, Dr. James Naismith, was trying to find something more interesting for his students to do during the winter months. So he nailed up two peach baskets on a balcony, which just happened to be ten feet high, at either end of a gym floor. There were eighteen players in the class, nine on a side. Dr. Naismith typed up a list of thirteen rules. The ball, a soccer ball, could be advanced by throwing or batting it with the hands. Players could not run with the ball but had to throw it from where they caught it. No physical contact was allowed. Dribbling was not introduced until some time later when a trapped player was allowed to throw the ball up and catch it. Floor dribbling came along even later.

It was an immediate success. Women started playing right away, in 1892. During the early years, scores were low, usually well under ten goals per game. Colleges picked it up after the turn of the century. The sport grew most rapidly in the Midwest.

Rules were standardized in the 1920s and 1930s. Free throws were no longer awarded for traveling violations, and the center jumps were no longer required after each goal. The game opened up. Fast breaks and other strategies made it a quicker game. The first national collegiate tournament, the National Invitational Tournament (N.I.T.) was played in 1938 (Temple 60, Colorado 36) and the NCAA tournament followed in 1939 (Oregon 46, Ohio State 33).

Professional basketball started early also, in New York and New Jersey, with local teams inviting teams from other towns. Leagues soon followed, developing from 1906-20. Out of interleague competition came the National Basketball Association in 1949. That year Minneapolis, led by the great George Mikan, defeated Syracuse for the championship, six games to two. Over the years, great superstars have won the hearts of fans, Kareem-Abdul Jabbar, Wilt Chamberlain, Bob Cousy, Bill Russell, Elgin Baylor,

Bob Pettit, Pete Maravich, Oscar Robertson, Rick Barry, Jerry Lucas, Magic Johnson, Michael Jordan, Larry Bird. There are so many more of them, the all-time greats of basketball.

THE RULES

Basketball is a simple game. Popular games have to be simple since complex rules always spoil the fun of things. Two teams of five players each try to score points by placing a 29 inch round inflated ball through an 18 inch diameter cylindrical hoop which is 10 feet from the ground at the end of a rectangular floor. They also endeavor to stop the opponent from doing the same at the other end of the floor. The ball can be advanced only by passing with the hands or by dribbling it on the floor. Play continues until the ball goes out of bounds or a goal (two points) is scored, in which case the ball goes to the opposite team. Play is also stopped upon a violation, the most common of which is walking without dribbling (award possession to opponent) or a foul − initiating physical contact with an opponent. Upon a foul, the ball is awarded to the other team, unless the fouled player was shooting, or unless the fouling team has accumulated six fouls, in which case the player may shoot free throws. Two free throws are awarded in the first instance, one-and-one in the second.

These are the essential rules of basketball. There are other frequently used rules which I'll cover, and some minor ones, which are in the glossary along with the jargon of the game. The official rules are set forth by the National Federation of State High School Associations, 11724 Plaza Circle, Box 20626, Kansas City, MO 64195. The rule book costs $2.75 plus $3.00 shipping.

Here are some rules which should be more commonly understood.

1. A player can only dribble with one hand at a time. Kids tend to bring the second hand to help out and that's a double dribble violation. Once a player ceases to dribble, she may not dribble again.

2. A closely guarded player can't hold or dribble the ball for more than five seconds or she loses it.

3. A player or team has ten seconds to bring the ball up court past the division (mid-court) line. Once the *ball and both feet* are past that line, the back court becomes out of bounds for the offense

Figure 33
BASKETBALL COURT DIAGRAM

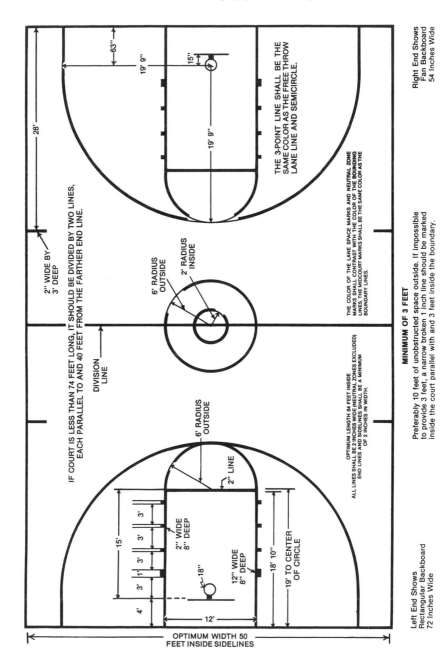

63"

19' 9"

15"

19' 9"

THE 3-POINT LINE SHALL BE THE SAME COLOR AS THE FREE THROW LANE LINE AND SEMICIRCLE.

28'

2" WIDE BY 3' DEEP

IF COURT IS LESS THAN 74 FEET LONG, IT SHOULD BE DIVIDED BY TWO LINES, EACH PARALLEL TO AND 40 FEET FROM THE FARTHER END LINE.

6" RADIUS OUTSIDE

2" RADIUS INSIDE

DIVISION LINE

THE COLOR OF THE LANE SPACE MARKS AND NEUTRAL ZONE MARKS SHALL CONTRAST WITH THE COLOR OF THE BOUNDING LINES. THE MIDCOURT MARKS SHALL BE THE SAME COLOR AS THE BOUNDARY LINES.

OPTIMUM LENGTH 84 FEET INSIDE ALL LINES SHALL BE 2 INCHES WIDE (NEUTRAL ZONES EXCLUDED) END LINES AND SIDELINES SHALL BE A MINIMUM OF 2 INCHES IN WIDTH.

MINIMUM OF 3 FEET

Preferably 10 feet of unobstructed space outside. If impossible to provide 3 feet, a narrow broken 1 inch line should be marked inside the court parallel with and 3 feet inside the boundary.

6" RADIUS OUTSIDE

2" LINE

15'

3'
3'
3'
3'
1'
3'

2" WIDE 8" DEEP

12" WIDE 8" DEEP

18'—

4'

12'

18' 10"

19' TO CENTER OF CIRCLE

OPTIMUM WIDTH 50 FEET INSIDE SIDELINES

Left End Shows Rectangular Backboard 72 Inches Wide

Right End Shows Fan Backboard 54 Inches Wide

for the remainder of that possession.

4. No part of an offensive player can remain within the offensive free throw lane for more than three seconds.

5. A player has only five seconds to inbound a ball, and except after a goal, he must inbound from the spot designated by the referee.

6. Five players must start a game but as few as two can finish it.

7. The 2-inch boundary lines around the court are out of bounds and neither the ball nor the foot may touch them when in possession of the ball.

8. A player may not touch a shot ball in downward flight or goal tending will be called and the points are awarded as if the shot had been made.

9. Players may not try to disconcert a free thrower. Once the free thrower has the ball no one may enter or leave a marked lane space. Players may not enter the free throw lane to rebound until the ball leaves the shooter's hand. The shooter may not enter the lane until the ball hits the rim or backboard.

10. *Principle of Verticalization.* Technically, a defensive player has a right to the space directly over him, and may jump straight up without fouling. However, most referees will nevertheless call a foul on the defender if contact is made. The best counsel at this point is to hold the ground, raise the hands, and stay still.

The size of a basketball court will vary depending on the age of the kids. Many middle schools have a gym about half the size of the usual 50' x 84' high school gym. By seventh or eighth grade, most schools, however, will have the larger size. See Figure 33, printed with permission from the National Federation of State High School Associations.

GLOSSARY – TALKING BASKETBALL

AIRBALL – An outside shot that misses the hoop, backboard, everything. At college games, you'll hear the fans razz a player who has shot an airball every time he gets his hands on the ball thereafter.

ARC – The path of a shot ball. A low arc is called a *brick*, a too high arc, a *rainmaker*. Ordinarily, an arc should be about 15 feet from the floor on a 15 foot jump shot.

BACKBOARD — The rectangular or semicircular fan-shaped surface on which the basket is mounted, used also for bank shots. It is also called the *glass*, if so constructed. In outside lots, it's usually made of wood or metal. The backboard has also been called a bankboard or a bangboard. (See Figure 34.)

Figure 34
BACKBOARD

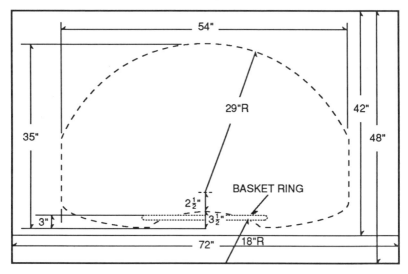

The backboard may be glass, wood, or metal 6 feet by 4 feet, or a 3.5 feet rectangle, or it may be a 54" wide fan with dimensions as shown above, according to National Federation rules

BACKCOURT — The half of the court where the ball isn't in play. In the early days, some players stayed back on defense all the time, by rule, and were called backcourt players. Now the term is used to described the area itself, and the offense can't take the ball into the backcourt area once they completely cross the mid-court line (also called the backcourt line).

BALL — Usually leather, the circumference must be 29 1/2 to 30 inches for boys and an inch less for girls. Weight is 20 to 22 ounces for boys, 2 ounces less for girls. It should be inflated to a pressure so that it will bound to a height of 49 to 54 inches at the top when dropped from over 6 feet high.

BANK SHOT — The ball hits the backboard before it goes in. Sometimes it's just a lucky shot, although the shooter will smile as though he intended to bank it.

BASELINE — The end-line boundary at each end of the court, under the hoop. A baseline drive is very effective if you can get by the defender. The baseline, however, is out of bounds.

BASKET — The 18-inch circumference *hoop* that we shoot at. Also known as a bucket. When the ball goes through, it is a *field goal* and one, two, or three points are awarded.

BLOCK — To *reject* or *repel* a shot ball before it hits the top of its arc. Usually, it is just called a *rejection*.

BOX-OUT — A defensive move using the back of the body to screen a player from getting a rebound.

CENTER — Usually the tallest player on the team. He or she plays underneath, in the lane, where the action is.

CHARGE — A player control foul committed by a driving offensive player hitting a defender who is stationary and who has established his position. The defense gets possession.

CIRCLE — An offensive move without the ball in which the player circles his defender to turn and confuse him and then breaks free for a pass.

CRASH — Running toward the hoop after a shot is taken to get a rebound, called crashing the boards.

CUT — Another move without the ball. The player dashes into or across the lane looking for a pass.

DEFENSE — The endeavor to get possession of the ball and prevent the opposition from scoring points.

DENY — The endeavor to prevent a player being open for a pass by blocking the passing lane with the body or at least an arm.

DOUBLE-TEAM — Two on one defense, usually in the corners, also called a trap. It also occurs by *fronting* and *backing* a big man underneath.

DRIBBLE — To advance the ball by bouncing it with either hand. The feet can do no more than a pivot move after a dribble. Once the dribble is stopped, it can't start again or a *double-dribble violation* is called. Dribbles can be *behind the back* or between the legs to keep the ball away from a defender.

DRIVE — A running dribble toward the hoop for a shot up close.

DUNK — A shot in which the player places the ball directly into the hoop, also called a slam, stuff, jam. If the player spins 180 degrees, it's a reverse slam. Watch Michael Jordan, he's the best ever at this. (See Figure 35.)

Figure 35
THE DUNK

Two handed slam dunk

FAKE — The art of getting a defender off balance or moving in one direction so you can move in another. The player usually moves the head or the ball, or even takes a step in one direction and then suddenly goes in another. A player can also fake a shot, called a pump *fake*, to get the defender to jump, and then the shooter goes up as the defender comes down. Players can put a series of fakes together to get a defender off balance.

FAST BREAK — Moving the ball up court quickly by virtue of a long pass to a player streaking up court. The defense never gets set. The team fast breaking uses their speed and needs endurance.

FLASH — Quick movements from one side of the free throw lane to the other, usually by a big player posting up at one side then flashing across the lane to the other.

FOLLOW-UP — Moving to the boards after taking a shot. Usually the player fades to the opposite side of the court from the shot since most rebounds bounce to the opposite side.

FORWARD − In the early days, these were offensive players who were allowed to move across the mid-court line and play offense. Now, the term refers to the tall players who take a position near the baseline on either side of the hoop. More and more these days, coaches just assign numbers to positions and areas.

FOUL − Illegal contact between two players with any part of the body. The player causing the contact gets the foul, the other team gets possession or a shot depending on the type of foul. A *personal foul* is contact with an opponent. A *common foul* is a personal foul which is neither flagrant, intentional, nor committed against a player trying for a field goal. An *intentional foul* is violent or savage. A *technical foul* is a non-contact foul. A *player contact foul*, also known as a charge, is committed by a ball handler.

FREE THROW − A free shot awarded to a player who is fouled. The shot is taken from the free throw line, 15 feet from the hoop.

FREE THROW LANE − The 12 foot wide area bounded by the free throw lines, also called the *paint, inside the lane*, or *underneath*. This area is where most of the action occurs in basketball.

FREEZE − A type of offense which patiently, slowly controls the ball, either to waste time on the clock or to wait for a high percentage shot. Pete Carril coaches that way at Princeton University. The scores are always low, and it's boring. The pros don't allow it; I don't like it.

FRONT − See DENY. There, the player blocks the passing lane with his body to deny a pass, usually to a big man underneath.

GAME − Usually four six-minute quarters in grammar school and four eight-minute quarters in high school with a ten-minute halftime. If the game ends in a tie, three-minute overtime quarters are played until one ends with a team ahead in score. Teams get four time outs per game and one additional for each overtime.

GIVE AND GO − The bread and butter play of basketball. A pass to a teammate, a dash toward the hoop past your defender, and a return pass for the lay-up. It's used far too infrequently.

GOOSENECK − The position of the hand and forearm after a shot, resembling a gooseneck.

GUARD − The name given to the players who bring the ball

up court. They used to be defensive players only, guarding the defensive area, not allowed past mid-court. The *point guard* is the play maker, a ball handler. The *off guard* is a shooting guard.

INBOUNDS — The playing area. A ball is passed from out of bounds after a field goal (a basket) or any time the ball goes out of bounds. A player has only five seconds to inbound and must start from the spot designated by the referee, except after a field goal.

JAB — A fake pivot step toward a defender to drive her back and get some room for a shot or pass. A reverse jab does the opposite, heading away from the basket and then breaking toward it. Also called a rocker step.

JUMP BALL — The opening play of the game. Two players meet at mid-court and the referee throws the ball up between them. They must tap it to teammates who are waiting outside the large mid-court circle. Jump shots used to occur whenever two opposing players were in equal possession of the ball, but now they just award it alternatively to either team (to speed up the game).

JUMP SHOT – See SHOTS.

JUMP STOP — A key play not often taught to kids, yet it's an essential of footwork. Whenever a moving player comes to catch a pass or a rebound, he should jump onto both feet on the balls of the toes, so that either foot can then be a pivot. It also sets up the balanced triple threat position.

KEY — The term used to designate the area including the free throw lane and the free throw circle. The top of the key, the point of the circle farthest from the hoop, is the area where most plays are initiated.

LAY-UP — See SHOTS.

LOB — A high pass over a defender, usually a fast break pass to a streaking guard or a pass over a defender fronting a player underneath.

MAN-TO-MAN — One-on-one defense, guarding a specific player instead of an area.

OFFENSE — The endeavor to score points by making field goals. A motion offense uses speed, screens, and shooting ability; a power offense looks for the big players underneath.

OFFICIALS — They make sure the game is played by the rules. Basketball officials are the most harassed people in all sports.

The game is fast and the fans are very close. This leads to much disagreement. The official referee signals of the National Federation of State High School Associations are reproduced in Figure 36.

OUTLET — A wing player, near the sideline, who sets up for a pass from a defensive rebounder. The idea is to set up away from any defenders so the rebounder can get the ball quickly out from underneath.

OVERSHIFT — Defending off center, to the strong side of a player. If a player is right-handed, we shift a bit to that side, placing the left foot forward blocking that lane.

PALM — The part of the hand that should touch the ball only rarely. Basketball is a finger game. In the early days, a palm ball was a violation if the hand made contact while dribbling with the underside of the ball.

PERIMETER — The outside edge of the normal shooting distance — normally about 17-19 feet from the hoop. In college ball, a basket from the 19 foot, 9 inch distance scores three points. In the pros, it's from 21 feet. This is called the three-point line.

PERIOD — A game is divided into four periods or quarters of 6 to 8 minutes each, depending on the level of play.

PICK — Screening a defender who is guarding a player with the ball so he can dribble around the defender.

PIVOT — Stepping and stretching in any direction with one foot, while the toes of the other foot are in continuous contact with the floor. The pivot foot can spin, but not lift or slide.

POINT — The area at the top of the key from which most plays commence.

POST — See Chapter 3. The area underneath the basket. This term also describes a move by which a big player screens his defender with his back while awaiting a pass, and then rolls to either side to score.

PRESS — Full-court defense. This is an endeavor to harass and frustrate the players bringing the ball up court. The pressure will, you hope, force a mistake leading to a turnover.

QUARTER — See PERIOD.

REBOUND — A missed shot which caroms off the rim or backboard onto the field of play. The attempt to secure this loose ball is called rebounding.

SCISSOR — A play whereby two offensive players criss-cross

Figure 36

NATIONAL FEDERATION OFFICIAL BASKETBALL SIGNALS

#	Signal
1	Start clock
2	Stop clock or do not start clock — plus 19 toward the table for radio/TV time-out
3	Stop clock for jump ball
4	Beckon substitute ball dead - clock stopped
5	Stop clock for foul
6	Technical foul
7	Blocking
8	Holding
9	Pushing or charging
10	Illegal use of hand
11	Player control foul
12	A. Intentional foul B. Double foul
13	Traveling
14	Illegal dribble
15	3 second violation *Open hand - run end line
16	Over and back or carrying the ball
17	Free throw, or designated spot violation
18	5 or 10 second violation - use both hands for 10
19	Direction signal (AND PLUS)
20	Designates out-of-bounds spot
21	No score
22	Goal counts or is awarded (OR)
23	Point(s) scored (use 1 or 2 fingers) (AND)
19	Direction signal (PLUS)
24	Bonus free throw for 2nd throw drop 1 arm - for 2 throws use 1 arm with 2 fingers *Free throw violation by B
25	Lack of Action Prior to Warning / After Warning / Point Toward Team Responsible
26	3-Point Field Goal Attempt / And If Successful

5 - 89

in front of a third player, usually at a high post.

SCREEN — Gaining a set position in a lane and thereby preventing a defender from moving thus freeing the player defended. Used interchangeably with the term *pick*, although screen often refers to a play off the ball.

SCRIMMAGE — A practice game, usually intra-squad.

SHIN SPLINTS — A common ailment involving pain in the shin area, sometimes quite painful. They often occur on harder surfaces or before a player is properly conditioned. Socks should always be worn at full height to keep this area warm.

SHOTS — There are many. The *lay-up* and *jump shot* are the dominant shots. *Chippies* are shots from directly underneath the net. *Set shots* are jump shots without a jump, usually from a far, undefended distance. A *foul shot* is a set shot. Underneath, we also have *hook shots* and *dunks*. Short jump shots often use the backboard in a *bank shot*. *Three point shots* are from about 19 feet 9 inches or farther away. A *fade away shot* is just that, a fading backward jump shot. Some shots get their name from the floor position from which the shot is taken, e.g., *corner, top of the key, half-court, high post*. A *double-pump* is a fake shot followed by a shot off a lay-up. Names of shots also vary a bit by region. But the bread and butter are the lay-ups and jumpers, and that's where your kid should start.

SHUFFLE — A motion or continuity pattern offensive play whereby all players continuously move according to a set pattern, looking for opportunities to score.

SOFT-TOUCH — A term used to identify short shots which softly hit the rim and drop in. They usually flow from good form, good ball control, and hand coordination.

SQUARE — Setting the shoulders perpendicular or slightly angled to the hoop before shooting. The idea is more one of balance and being set.

STALL — Boring! This is an attempt to waste time by passing around the perimeter. Some teams use it to slow down the tempo or keep the score close against a better team. It used to be allowed forever so the shot clock was instituted to require a team to shoot in 24 seconds in the pros or 45 seconds in college games. There is no shot clock in youth basketball. Stalling is just not basketball!

STRONG SIDE — Often, especially against a zone defense,

teams will place an extra man to one side. This also happens naturally on the side the ball is on.

SUPERMAN — A drill for shooting or rebounding consecutively and alternatively from each side of the basket, back and forth.

SWITCH — A defensive move when two offensive players criss-cross or pick and roll; they switch and guard each other's man.

TEN SECONDS — The amount of time given to inbound and bring the ball past mid-court after a change of possession.

TIP — To tap the ball to another player or toward the hoop without catching it. Used often to steal passes or tap rebounds.

TRAILER — A player who follows a driving ball handler to the hoop. He will often shout "trailer" to alert the player that he is ready for a dump pass backward or a rebound.

TRANSITION — The change from offense to defense or vice versa. Quickness and alertness here can make a difference.

TRAP — Double teaming a player with the ball, usually in a corner or along the sideline.

TRAVEL — To take two steps without dribbling.

TRIPLE THREAT — The balanced offensive or defensive stance from which a player can move in any direction with equal ease.

TURNOVER — Losing possession to the other team while dribbling or because of a bad pass.

UNDERNEATH — Home to the big players under the hoop. The heartland of basketball.

WALKING — Taking two steps without a dribble.

ZONE — The poor man's defense. The zone defense is not as skillful as the man-to-man, trying more to clog up the area closest to the basket, thus forcing outside shots.

5.

BASKETBALL POSITIONS

COMPOSITION OF THE TEAM

Only five players from each team are on the floor at any one time. Youth teams usually range from twelve to eighteen players. This means a lot of kids either won't make the team or won't get much playing time. Fortunately, below sixth or seventh grade, and sometimes up to high school age, many towns run clinic or in-town recreation programs so anyone who wants to play can do so. Some of these clinics limit team size and require equal time or at least a certain minimum time for all players. I like this because very often the kids who are starting varsity in high school are not the ones who were the best at the grammar school level. Some kids get height and/or coordination much later than others; some practice much harder over the years and win out over a more natural athlete.

The oldest adage is that basketball is a big man's game. This is certainly not always the case at the youth level, but there is no question that height helps a lot when defending or shooting underneath, and the highest percentage shots *are* underneath. But, when you get down to it, that's about all you need height for. Rebounding has more to do with positioning than height. Also, at the young ages, the height differential is usually less than for adults. The point I'm making is that you should not discourage your child from playing basketball if he or she is not tall. It's a game they can enjoy for their entire life, urge them to learn it.

So while height is a very important element, speed, agility, leadership, a good outside shot, good dribbling, good passing, aggressiveness, quickness, and other attributes are all part of what's needed. Often, the tall guys have only their height and are otherwise less coordinated since they grow so fast. Believe me, I know, I was one of them.

I must repeat, basketball is a game you can play all your life. I've played it all of my life, and still do. It's a great game, good exercise, and a super way to get to meet people. (See Figure 33.) All sizes of people can play. Tall people may be able to contribute more, but there is a place for everyone. At the very best, encourage your child to hang in there and get some coaching and team play for a few seasons. Even if he is not playing much, he is practicing and learning the game. This experience will help him to get involved in playground pickup games, something he can do for the rest of his life.

Generally in basketball the taller players play underneath the hoop or along the baseline, center or forward, and shorter players fill the guard positions, where speed is more important. Let's discuss each position. There are one center, two forwards, and two guards on the floor. However, nowadays more and more teams tend to get away from the traditional designations, using numbers or floor positions to designate players.

THE CENTER

The tallest kid on the team will usually play at the center position. His or her area is mainly in the paint, under the hoop. The main job of the center on offense is to get open for the pass underneath and take the high percentage shot. They *must* be able to catch the ball! Centers also look to pick off defenders from teammates, who then can drive for a shot. Finally, they look for offensive rebounds and try to score with them. Defensively, the center's main job is to clog up the middle, preventing the opponents from taking shots underneath. A most important job is getting defensive rebounds. Centers must *always* look to box out or screen an opponent while rebounding.

On *offense*, the center's most effective weapon is the *post-up*.

In this position, the center stands with her back to the hoop and the defender. She has her arms outstretched for a pass, leaning slightly into the defender. This effectively screens the defender from stealing a pass to center, and also allows the center to *put a move* on the defender to get a shot off. *Posting-up* is particularly effective when the center is taller than the defender.

A player heads to the low post, the area by the large block next to the foul line under the hoop area. He feels the defender on his posterior, and keeps him in between his elbows, using the elbows and hands to feel the defender, even to control him a bit. The post player must make himself *feel wide*, working his way backward without fouling. If the defender is square, directly behind, he needs to get him to one side. Once a defender is to one side, he makes the move to the other side, moving hard, pivoting around the defender *as if he were a post*, not dribbling (or no more than one dribble) and then exploding upward. Don't throw the elbow, but keep it out for protection and to pick up a possible foul. Employ body and shot fakes as needed.

Perhaps the best move out of a low post is to head and shoulder fake to the inside, that is toward the foul lane, and then to *drop step* quickly the other way. A drop step is simply a step back with the baseline foot and a spin for the shot. This move anticipates that the defender will initially go with the first fake. It is essentially a pivot backward and a shot off the dropped foot. Of course, if the defender is already to one side, then no fake is needed and the player just drop steps the other way. The drop step can be used on either side of the lane, and can be used for an inside or an outside pivot.

Given all of the above, it makes sense for the center to regularly practice all of the moves which can be made from a post position. The most probable shots are usually to move to the left (from a post on the right side) for a lay-up, a hook shot, or a fading short jump-shot (see Chapter 3 on *Shooting*). In setting up the move, the center needs to develop fakes − fake right/go left, fake left/go right. (See Figure 36.) The footwork of the move from the post is important and needs to be practiced. Remember, big players use power from the post position and smaller players must rely more on speed, positioning, and fakes. Practice accordingly. (See Figure 37.)

A common bad habit of centers is the natural tendency to put

Figure 37
POSTING UP

Keep defender in the elbows, backing up as ball is about to be passed

Fake to one side, feet do not move

Drop step left foot, and quickly spin that way

Turn and hook. Make this move either way, either side

the ball down or dribble it underneath. The pivot step is often enough to do whatever needs to be done, even out of a low post. Sure, there are times a single dribble is needed to effect a fake, or to get closer to the hoop, but more often than not, the need for the dribble is just a failure to use the pivot step properly. Dribbling underneath is an invitation to have the ball stolen or bobbled in what is usually very heavy traffic.

If your child is a center, let him or her play one-on-one against you from the post position. It's great experience. Watch the walks!

The post positions are generally along the foul line. Up by the free throw line, it is called a *high post*. Close to the basket it is called a *low post*. Remember when posting that the foot cannot be inside the three second area for three seconds or there will be a violation. These violations drive coaches crazy. It's okay to slide in and out of the position to avoid the violation. (See Figure 38.)

A low-post position sets up center shots. A high post position is used for play making, picks, give and gos, and many other plays discussed more fully in Chapter 6.

Centers *must* know how to shoot hook shots, and *should* learn to shoot left-handed underneath. These shots were treated in

Figure 38
FLOOR POSITIONS

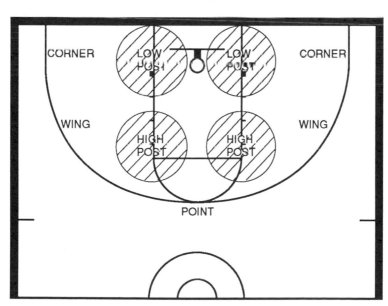

Chapter 3. If your child is tall, urge him to practice underneath the hoop, in the paint. Sure, he should practice outside shots, they are part of the game and he will need them to be a fully rounded player. But, unless he has a great outside shot, his team will need him underneath and that's where the coach will tell him to stay. So emphasize short jump shots, lay-ups, hook shots, chippies, using both hands, fakes, fake pumps, tap-ins, using the pivot step, avoid dribbling — this is what they will need to perfect.

Defensively, the center is expected to dominate the paint area and keep the opponents from shooting the high-percentage underneath shots. This involves fronting — getting the body or a hand in front of an opponent trying to post up underneath — in order to prevent the pass underneath. It also involves blocking shots and otherwise harassing anyone driving into the paint area.

Centers usually pick up a lot of fouls, particularly at young ages. This is because there is a lot of action and traffic underneath and also because of inexperience. Blocking shots takes height or leaping ability, because the ball should be blocked far enough from the shooter to avoid a foul. Also, the preferred technique is to block *across* the ball, not *toward* the shooter, to minimize the chance for a foul. Whenever two kids go up very close to each other, chances are there will be some body contact. If the defensive player is moving, or is off the ground and *any* body contact is made, a foul will be called. So your child must know that unless he can dominate the shooter, the best technique underneath is just to stand still with arms raised straight up, trying to put *some* pressure on the shot or even draw an offensive foul. If the defender is still and contact is made, then it's an offensive foul or *charge*. The best defense against a player driving for a lay-up is to establish position in front of that player, stay still, and take the offensive charge.

Perhaps the most important defensive responsibility of the center is to get defensive rebounds. If the other team gets the rebound, it's an easy shot and two points. Therefore, it's essential for the defensive team to get rebounds. Also, since defenders are usually positioned between their opponents and the hoop, they should be in better position to get the rebound.

A key defensive strategy is to *box out* the opponent as a shot is taken. The idea here is, upon release of a shot by an opponent, to hesitate a second before turning to face the hoop for the re-

Figure 39
BOXING OUT

*Here both defenders underneath and the one by the
free throw line are boxing out their men*

bound. The hesitation allows the defender to see which direction
the opponent will take to get the rebound. We then just step in his
way. Rotate the back to him after he is blocked off. Stick the
posterior into the opponent and outstretch the arms a bit to make it
tough for him to get around. It's called making oneself wide. (See
Figure 39.) Once the center gets the rebound, he looks to the
sideline for a teammate, usually a guard, known as the *outlet*, and
passes to him. We'll discuss this more in Chapter 6.

FORWARDS

Forwards are also taller players, usually the next tallest after
the center. They need to be tall because they are also frequently
called upon to play underneath the hoop. However, forwards also
cover the wing area and the corners of the court, so they need to
develop an outside shot, preferably a baseline shot, and they need

to be able to dribble and pass. Each position requires some skills unique to that position. For forwards, it's the corner shot and the baseline drive. Of course, forwards need to be complete players and need to develop all skills of the game, but they should emphasize the skills most often required of them. This is where the parent can be most helpful, assisting in the practice of those special skills. Forwards spend a lot of time in the corner or baseline area, and they want to perfect skills from that perspective.

On offense the first duty of the forward, besides following the steps required of pattern plays, is to get free for a pass. Most teams will have a series of plays, or a normal offensive routine, requiring the forward to catch a pass from the guard, or to cut or make some moves underneath. However, many offensive routines start with a pass to the corner, to the forward.

So the forward wants to develop a *move* which frees her up for such a pass. The best move is to fake a run to the center, taking a few quick steps toward the center, and then quickly dart back to the corner for the pass. The idea, as stated earlier, for any fake is to *relate* to the defender. Once the defender is committed, then dart back the other way. (See Figure 40.)

When the forward gets the ball, she simply follows the routine of the offense. Usually there will be someone moving to the hoop for a possible pass or the center will post-up low for a pass. Someone may come out to pick the defender who is guarding the forward. Otherwise, the forward may need to make her own way, fake outside and drive the baseline, or jab step and take a jump shot. If all else fails, pass the ball back out to a guard and start another offensive series.

Perhaps the strongest skill needed by forwards is passing. They very often get the ball in the corner, too far away to shoot. They need to be able to pass the ball effectively and this should be practiced. The two hand overhead pass to the low post is one such pass. Forwards are also called upon to play under the hoop, so all skills mentioned for centers – posting, hook shots, boxing out, fronting a player, avoiding fouls, taking charges, and rebounding – must be practiced, offense and defense.

Unique to the forward position on defense is the baseline drive. (See Figure 41.) Forwards never want an opponent to drive inside them successfully, between them and the baseline. If that oc-

Figure 40
CORNER JAB

Here the corner player takes some sharp steps inside, to get the defender in motion

Then he suddenly darts back to the corner for the pass

curs, the likelihood of a score increases dramatically for the opponents. Always close off the baseline drive with the leg closest to the baseline. There's always more help available in the other direction. The forward also needs to guard against the fake shot and drive. There is a strong natural tendency to try to block outside shots, and the *fake shot and drive* move is usually very successful at younger ages. We'll discuss this all more generally in Chapter 7 on *Defense*. We'll also talk then about how best to defend the outside shot.

GUARDS

In 1988, I used to enjoy going to watch Trenton State College games. A friend of mine had a son on the team, and they had a good shot at the Division III National Championship. The team also had a 5 foot, 7 inch guard named Greg Grant who eventually broke the all time National scoring record for collegiate careers with over 2600 points. Greg was the ultimate guard, and a wonder to behold.

Guards are usually the shorter players on the team. However,

Figure 41
BASELINE DRIVE

*Defender never got leg out to protect the baseline,
allowing the corner forward to drive the line*

keep in mind that in the pros, the guards are often about 6 feet, 4 inches tall. It's all relative. The biggest guys are usually needed underneath (the seven footers!).

Guards need to dribble. They need to be able to take on a defender one-on-one and dribble around him. If a team can't get the ball down the court, they will fail miserably. At young ages, local rules often require the defense to wait until the ball crosses the mid-court line before they can attack the ball, and this is a welcome rule. However, guards still need to be able to dribble effectively with both hands. This is what they must emphasize in personal practice. They can practice anywhere, and they don't need a basketball court. I said this in Chapter 1, and I repeat it here. Dribbling is the most effective skill in basketball and the one which you, as a parent, should emphasize to your child. If she can dribble, she will be more valuable. It's a skill that can be learned and improved with practice. Guards *must* learn to dribble. Practice one-on-one. Have your child dribble while you try to steal the ball. It's the best practice a guard can have. Guards need to be able to dribble in close quarters, in heavy traffic, and they need to be able to speed dribble, at a dead run. (See Figure 42.) The kid on the team who can dribble the best will be called upon to bring the ball up the floor.

After dribbling, guards need to be able to pass the ball. They need to be able to pass deceptively, accurately, and with strength and speed on the ball. We discussed passing in Chapter 2. The key is to know where your teammates are, to be able to dribble with your head up and eyes scanning the play, and to spot the open teammate. The kid who can do this best will be the *point guard*.

They are the quarterbacks. He sets up at the top of the key and starts the offensive play. Guards also need to be able to shoot outside and drive inside. These are not as important as dribbling and passing, but shooting ability always helps. Usually, a team has one good outside shooter and that's all you really need. If your child can develop such a shot, then practice it with them. A shooting guard is called an *off guard* and they usually play the wing area, between the guard and forward area. They generally have a favorite spot, where they can shoot the best, so that's where they hang out.

Figure 42
A GUARD ON THE RUN

Guards need to be able to move in traffic and, as here,
take advantage of any screens

Defensively, guards need to be able to steal passes. A kid who can steal passes is very valuable to the team because a stolen pass usually leads to an easy score. Chapter 7 deals with this skill in more detail. Guards want to be able to pressure the outside shooter, but more important, they want to ensure that the ball carrier doesn't drive by them. The key to good defense, as discussed above, is to prevent penetration. Keep the opponent away from the closer high percentage shots.

6.

OFFENSE

CONCEPTS VS. PLAYS

As a parent, you can help your child a lot by teaching offensive *concepts*. The coach will have his own set of plays for the team, but offensive *concepts* are the same everywhere. In this chapter, we will discuss these concepts and review some specific offensive skills. You and your youngster should review them together. Most kids don't know anything but pass and shoot, and an early understanding of concepts will go a long way. It will get your kid some extra playing time and that so necessary experience. This chapter will also include specific plays, so you can understand types of offensive patterns. Coaches could use these for their teams too.

Basketball is somewhere between football and soccer in play making. Football has very specific plays for all players to follow, while soccer has fewer plays, as such, and the game flows more according to a set of concepts and the opportunities of the moment. Basketball uses *both* plays and concepts, and both are equally employed. A *concept*, for instance, is that we can help get players free to shoot by screening away the defender. A *play* is the specific plan which sets up that screen. There are obviously several different ways to do it. We could use several different players for the screen, but the *concept* is always the same. Kids need to understand concepts, and if they do they can often make their own plays, tailored to the immediate situation. Also, understanding concepts helps them to understand what the coach is trying to do.

OFFENSIVE ZONES

The area in the offensive end of the court can be divided into five zones – the low post, high post, point, wing, and corner. (See again Figure 38.) The rectangular area under the basket, between the free throw lines, is called the lane or the paint. It is also called the three-second zone. There are small squares on either side of the free throw lines under the hoop called the blocks. Two more lines, called free throw stripes, are painted at intervals of three feet. Different coaches may have different terms, if so, your child will need to learn them. Language varies across the country. The free throw or foul line is the diameter of a circle which, with the foul lane, is called the key (it looks sort of like a keyhole). The end line of the court is called the baseline, and the mid-line of the court is also called the backcourt line. Offensive zones are often assigned numbers by the coach.

OFFENSIVE CONCEPTS

The high-percentage shot. You got to put the ball in the hoop! The bottom line of basketball is the final score. The team with the most points wins. We can debate about how important it is to win, and I'll certainly argue that sportsmanship must be the goal of youth athletics. It gripes me to see grammar school coaches playing the same kids all the time, sacrificing the development and confidence of the substitutes for a winning score. But the players who put the most points on the board will always see the most action. Good scorers are rare, they can't be kept on the bench!

There are a lot of aspects of scoring and we have talked about many of them. Offense grows out of defense, so scoring starts with a defensive rebound or a steal. It includes being able to control the ball through good passing and while bringing it up the floor. But, in the final analysis, scoring comes from good shooting and good shot selection.

This means that we need kids who can shoot, but more important, it means that we have to get them into a position for a high percentage shot, *a shot as close to the hoop as possible and relatively free of defensive pressure.* The way to get the open shot is a combination of speed, screening, faking, quickness, and a lot of motion.

Each coach will have his or her own system. They will have a series of offensive plays within the context of an overall offensive strategy. The best strategy is usually to try to get the ball safely into the hands of the big guys underneath, or to pick off a defender so someone, usually one of the better shooters, has an open jump shot. The plays are designed to get all players moving in a pattern designed to break up, frustrate, and confuse the defense. The whole idea is to free someone up for a high percentage shot.

Get it to the post man. The highest percentage shots are right underneath, in the *low post* area. The bread and butter play of basketball is a pass to the big players underneath, posting up their defenders. If a team has a good, big center who knows how to post effectively, and who can make power moves underneath, that's about all a team needs. It's basketball heaven! Chapter 4 discussed posting techniques. A bit later on, we will review the plays needed to get a good pass to the low post, and to get the post man free underneath. But the concept is to get the ball safely passed to a post player. See further discussion in Chapter 5 on the post play.

Attack from the wing. The real attack does not start from the point. The point is like a hinge on a door, feeding the ball to the wing. This point is usually too far from the low post to get a good pass in to that area. Likewise, the corner is not the optimum place to start our attack since a player can easily get trapped in the corner. The wing area is the quarterback zone for the actual attack. The great majority of passes from the point are to the wing area, and that's where the real action starts. The wing man, usually an off guard or a shooting forward, can either make an individual move, shoot or drive, or she can pass to the post, to the corner, or back out to the point. (See Figure 43.)

Pick and roll. The workhorse play of offense is the pick or screen. It's the best method used to free a player from their defender. The terms are pretty much used interchangeably anymore, although traditionally it's called a pick if the player to be freed *has* the ball, and it's a screen if the idea is to free up someone so she can *get* the ball.

The screening technique is fairly simple. You run up to the side of the player to be picked, preferably from a bit behind so she doesn't see you coming. Timing is important. If you approach too early, the defender will have time to avoid you, if you approach too

Figure 43
ATTACK FROM THE WING

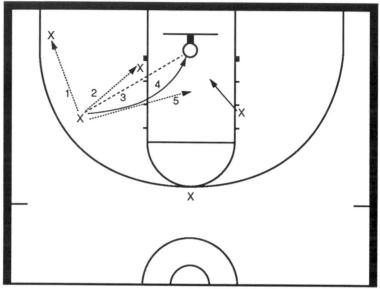

The wing can (1) pass to the corner, (2) pass to the
post, (3) shoot, (4) drive to the hoop, or (5) pass to the
other wing cutting the lane

late, you risk a foul by running into the defender.

Once there, spread the legs to make yourself wide, and keep the elbows out but hands in close by the chest to avoid a foul. Brace yourself because the defender is likely to bang into you, and referees will rarely call a foul, unless it's flagrant. (See Figure 44.)

I play a lot of small three-on-three games near my home, and I *always* look to pick the defender from the player with the ball. It either frees him to dribble or shoot, or it sets up a *pick and roll*. This is another bread-and-butter move, and your child must learn to appreciate its value. It always amazes me when I play to see some guys who never pick a defender. They stand around looking, and it never occurs to them to get involved. *They never learned the concept*, the pick is one of the two or three most basic offensive moves.

The *pick and roll* means that as soon as one picks the defender, he pivots or rolls in the same direction his teammate is moving, and moves parallel to him, with hand up, expecting a pass. Usually, this

Figure 44
THE PICK

Player with ball is guarded

Teammate comes over to pick defender, and opens lane for a drive

picked defender is out of the play so there is a two-on-one situation with the remaining defender. Often, the picker will be free, since his defender switches to pick up the dribbler. If so, then the picker rolls toward the basket for an easy pass and shot. (See Figure 45.)

Often, a player can play out at the high post in a stationary position and a guard will dribble close to her and use her as a pick. If the pick is successful in freeing the ball handler, then the picker can roll behind the dribbler. In this case, the picker becomes a *trailer* and can get a rebound.

Give and go. This is the best move in basketball. It doesn't involve a screen, just pure speed. A player simply passes to a teammate, and *as he passes*, he darts forward, explodes forward, past his defender, and looks for a quick return pass. If done right, it often leads to an easy lay-up. If your child learns to look for the give and go, he will catch the coach's eye, and the crowd will voice its approval also. The give and go works very well at young ages. It goes without saying that the player must also look to be the middleman on a give and go, to receive the pass and give it back quickly.

Figure 45
PICK AND ROLL

*If the second defender comes over to guard, the
picker rolls to the hoop . . .*

. . . and receives the pass for an easy lay-up.

The *concept* here is that it is often tough to dribble around an opponent, but it is very easy to run by her. The give and go allows this. It allows the player to get herself open for a quick return pass and a high percentage shot. (See Figure 46.)

Don't be too quick to dribble. Kids get a bad habit of dribbling too quickly after receiving a pass. However, once you put the ball down, you forgo other options. There is no need to rush, take a look inside, look for an opportunity. Obviously, if there is an opening or some space in front, you should advance the ball. But, if guarded, don't put the ball down too quickly. Dribbling is only one of the initial opportunities. The best players are looking for the opportunities even before they get the ball.

Individual moves. Basketball is a team sport first and foremost. Championships are rarely won with just one good player. However, the individual player also must be able to do things on his own. The coach will look at the numbers: points, rebounds, steals, assists, turnovers. The kids with numbers are going to play more. A lot of kids hardly ever get their hands on the ball, and then quickly get rid of it, passing it off. It seems they don't even want the ball. Be patient if one of these kids is yours; remember that most parents go through it at some point. Only a few kids are stars. However, your child must learn a few individual moves, and a few will quickly lead to more as the player within blossoms forth. I firmly believe that most kids have an athlete inside them, they can *all* improve. It just takes some desire, some faith, some encouragement, and a few ideas.

Your child won't get the ball passed to her if a defender is closely guarding her. She's got to find a way to get open. There are two good ways to do that individually, without the help of another teammate's screen.

One is a *jab step*. We touched on this in Chapter 3. The player steps *toward* the defender and then suddenly and quickly stops and comes back to her original position. The defender will tend to back up a bit at first, and so gets her weight going backward, off balance. Usually, the jab step will get a player open for a good second or so. It's enough. Another method is the *circle*. Just revolve or circle around the defender for a half or full circle. It confuses him, gets him off balance, and the player can then quickly dart out for a pass before the defender can recover.

Timing is always important. The player needs to sense when a teammate will look his way to pass, and try to get open at that time. Timing will come with experience.

Another way to get open is simply to get on the move. A key to

Figure 46
GIVE AND GO

Point passes ball to wing   *Point goes toward hoop*

Wing returns ball to driving point

offensive play is motion. With motion, a player will get open at some point. Players need to *cut* into the lanes, *flash* from one side of the lane to another, or sneak behind the hoop, along the baseline, and come in *through the back door*. The *back door* concept is based on the fact that defensive players are usually looking up court, and may not see someone slipping in from behind. The worst thing to do is just stand around!

Getting open is just the first step. Then we have to catch the pass. We discussed in Chapter 2 the need to *move to the ball* and *reach out* with the hands for the pass. This will avoid many steals. Always look for and anticipate the pass.

When moving to get a pass, a player should *jump stop*. This means that he simply jumps to the ball and lands on both feet. From this position, he can pivot on either foot. If the feet touch the ground unevenly, only the first foot to touch can be the pivot. (See Figure 47.)

When an open player catches a pass within her shooting range, especially within 12 feet of the hoop, *the first thought must be to shoot*. That's the name of the game. High percentage shots must be taken quickly. Even poor shooters have a good chance to sink a short jumper. Don't hesitate! Don't think! Just shoot very quickly before a defender comes on. At that range, we don't have much time, only a fraction of a second. How often do we hear the fans groan when an unsure kid fails to take a short jump shot? Players must learn to think about scoring.

Once the shot is off, unless the coach instructs that player to stay back to stop a fast break, the player must *follow the shot*. About one in six rebounds will bound back toward the shooter, and a good follow-up move will get many of them. Offensive rebounds are usually those that bounce out a good distance, since defensive players usually have the best position for short rebounds.

That's the ticket individually. Get open, catch the pass, fake, drive, shoot, and rebound. Make the moves, make it happen. Challenge yourself! Encourage your child to do these things.

OFFENSIVE PLAYS

Now we take the concepts and the individual moves and put them all together into a *play*. Actually, every single movement in a basketball game can be called a play. Give and go, screen, pick and roll, jab, flash, baseline drive — these are all plays. The best players make their own plays, within the structure of the team's overall offensive motion. The best plays are not necessarily the ones called by the coach or signalled by the point guard as he dribbles down court.

Figure 47
JUMP STOP

Jump to the pass. Then either foot can be used for a pivot

The best plays are those that seize the opportunity of the moment: a defender off balance or out of position, a height mismatch, an open lane.

However, it's also important that the overall movement of the offensive players be orderly and consistent. We want to keep players moving. Young players often get mesmerized by the action and tend to stand around and watch their teammates. It's also helpful to the passer to know ahead of time where her teammates are going to be. These plays are called patterns or continuous motion offenses. They are often a series of plays, designed to set players in motion in a pattern using screens or speed to get someone open for the high percentage shot. If no player is open, the play continues to move players around until someone is free, or until someone *makes it happen*. At any time, a player may seize an opportunity. All players, while running the pattern, should look for an opportunity to score or hit an open player.

These play patterns are usually very simple. A young team employs only one or two such patterns. The coach should have one in mind; if not, show him or her this chapter.

The shuffle is probably one of the most widely used play patterns in basketball. I learned it as a kid, and I've seen it many times since then. In this pattern, the players set up and move to the positions shown in Figure 48 as the point guard (#1) reaches the top of the key. The off guard (#2) shuffle cuts into and across the lane, cutting close for a screen from a forward positioned at the high post (#3). In the first diagram, the point guard looks to pass to the cutting off guard who then drives to the basket or dishes the ball off to one of the big players underneath (#4, #5). If, however, the point can't get the ball to #2, he looks, in the second diagram, for #4 who then flashes across the lane behind #2. If that doesn't work out, then in the third diagram, #1 uses #3 as a screen and dribbles into the lane, or dishes it off to #3. If nothing looks good, #1 just passes off to #5, who comes out to the wing, #3 heads to the point, and #1 then heads to the spot vacated by #4. Note that the pass to #5 in the wing is a good give and go opportunity for #1. If nothing worked, then the ball is passed by #5 back to #3 at the point and the play is run again from the opposite side. By then, the players are in place for another shuffle. The players must *all* know how to move from *each* position. It seems like a lot to know, but that's what practice is for. The point is that all players are constantly in motion all over the floor, creating opportunities. Usually the pattern needs to be run only once or twice before an opportunity is created or before a player tries to make something happen. This play is called a continuity pattern. If it fails, the team is already set up to run it the other way.

Scissor. This is another common play, although it's not a continuous pattern. Two guards bring the ball up court and as they approach the key, the center moves to the high post. He receives the ball and the guards criss-cross in a scissor move in front of him. The center may give it to either guard as they pass in front of him. If not, he turns to face the hoop and may again look either to pass to the off guard or dribble or shoot himself. The forwards can also post-interchange underneath, creating another passing opportunity. The point guard circles and returns to the point for a pass back out if the play fails. (See Figure 49.)

Post-interchange. We talked earlier about getting the ball to the wing and then trying to pass it to the big player posting up underneath. Another option is to have two big players line up on the opposite low post blocks and then switch positions. (See Figure 50.) The player moving away from the ball (#4) stops momentarily under the hoop to screen the oncoming defender #2. The center, #5, is now free for a pass underneath and should, in the best case, get

Figure 48
THE SHUFFLE

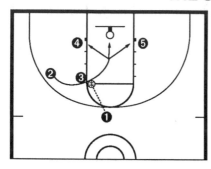

First movement: #2 cuts around the high post #3 and drives to shoot or to dish off to #4 or #5

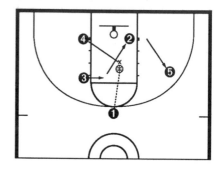

If #2 doesn't get the pass, then #4 immediately cuts behind him and looks for a pass. If no pass is open then #3 starts to float across, and #5 drifts to the wing

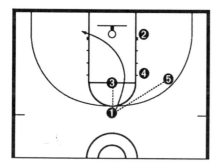

#1, still with the ball, shuffle cuts around #3's screen, or passes to #3 or to #5

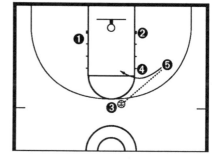

If nothing else worked, then #5 passes back to the point, taken by #3, and the floor is now set for a shuffle the other way. #5 begins by cutting around #4's pick

the ball just as she reaches the screen. The screening player is always closest to the baseline so the receiving player can get the pass.

Fast break. This play starts back with the defensive rebound. (See Figure 51.) The rebounder, #5, turns and immediately passes to an *outlet*, #3, on the sideline. The key is for a guard always to be

Figure 49
THE SCISSOR

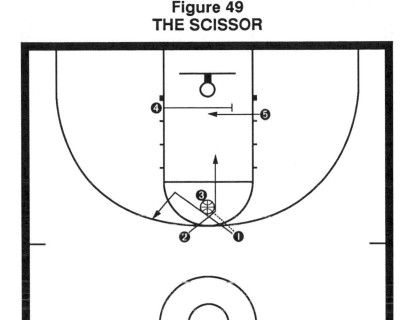

#1 passes to #3 at a high post. #2 quickly cuts by #3 for a hand-off. #1 also cuts by for a hand-off, but cuts out if he doesn't get the ball. #3 can either hand off to one of the guards, or turn and shoot or drive. He also can pass to #5 underneath. If nothing is open he passes out to #1

there. The guard on the ball side of the court usually has the responsibility to head to the same spot on every rebound and be ready for the outlet pass. As the ball is passed to the outlet the three other players head to three fast break lanes down the middle and opposite sides of the court. The outlet breaks up court looking to pass quickly to his teammate in the center lane. This play requires speed, endurance, speed dribbling, and the ability to make a lay-up at full throttle. The ball handler drives up mid-court and looks to pass to the sideline breakers as they move to the hoop.

Outside pick and roll. A nice play I've seen in youth basketball has the point guard, #1, pass to a shooting forward, #3. (See Figure 52.) Then the point darts to the high post and picks the player defending, the off guard, #2. The off guard cuts around the screen into the lane for the ball. She can either drive or dump off to the rolling point guard.

Man-to-man or Zone? Motion patterns such as the shuffle work best against man-to-man defense. Screens, the give and go, pick and roll, and jab moves work against anything. However, a zone is a tough defense to get inside against. As we will discuss later, the zone is sometimes banned in youth basketball so that the kids learn real defense. It's banned in the pros too. It's just not basketball. However, it is easy for kids to learn and if it can be used. It's popular with coaches because it's so simple.

A zone forces outside shooting. The reason is defensive players essentially bunch up around the lane. This defense more easily allows defenders to *front* the big offensive players underneath and deny passes to them. It also is hard to drive into the congestion of defenders.

Cutting into the lane, into the gaps of the zone, is one way to *split* the zone. It requires a good hard passer to thread the needle with crisp passes. Post-interchange plays also work well against a

Figure 50
POST INTERCHANGE

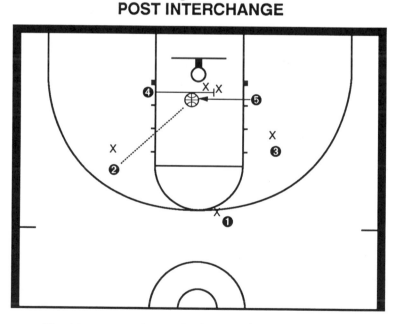

The big men underneath should always try to screen for each other. The player closest to the ball cuts to the middle and screens the other man's defender

Figure 51
THREE LANE FAST BREAK

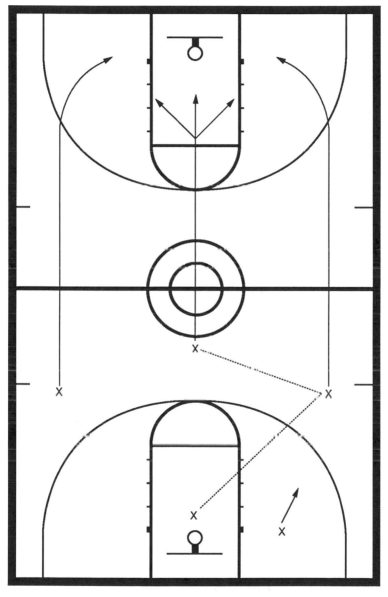

*Rebounder underneath passes to outlet, who passes
to midcourt. Two wide players streak up sideline, and
all three angle for the hoop*

Figure 52
OUTSIDE PICK AND ROLL

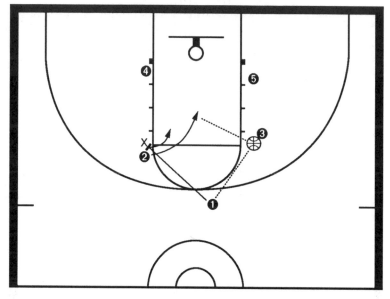

#1 passes to #3 and then proceeds to screen for #2.
The pick and roll is on

zone. Usually, teams try to overload a zone to one side. Players give each other screens to provide for short outside shots, pick and roll, or give and go plays.

A nice offense to use against a zone is a *wheel* type motion. It not only overloads the zone, but it keeps everyone in motion also. (See Figure 53.) Here, the players line up in point (#1), two wings (#2, #3), and two forwards (#4, #5). The first motion is a pass from point to #3 wing. The wing is free to drive or shoot. If nothing is available, the second motion is wing to corner. This can work as a give and go back to the wing who cuts to the hoop. The wing can also set up in a low post for a pass from the corner. Otherwise, in the third motion, the wing screens for #4 who flashes across the lane. The corner may hit #4, or give it back to #1, who has moved into the wing. Everyone revolves like a wheel, #2 goes to point, #3 goes to opposite wing, #4 returns to forward, and everyone is set up for the same or another play.

Figure 53
WHEEL MOTION

In this set, point passes to #3 who looks to shoot or drive

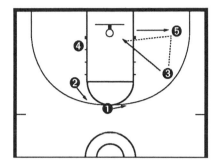

If she can't drive, #3 passes to the corner and looks for a give-and-go or a pass to the low post. As soon as #3 moves, #2 and #1 begin to turn the wheel

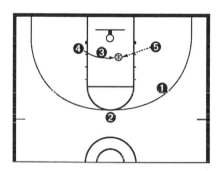

If #5 can't get the ball to #3, then #3 picks for #4 who flashes the lane

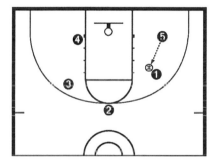

If nothing works, then back to #1 to start over again

7.
DEFENSE

DEFENSIVE CONCEPTS

The images most associated with basketball are those of Michael Jordan twisting high in the air for a reverse slam dunk, or Larry Bird popping in a three-pointer. However, more and more, we herald the quickness of a Spud Webb stealing a pass or a Patrick Ewing jam stuffing an attempted shot.

It's called defense. You need to talk to your child about its importance. Kids often play poorly on defense. They fail to stay between their opponent and the hoop. They allow players to drive around them. They are easily faked out. They miss opportunities to steal the ball by not being alert. These are the four main errors kids make, so make sure your child understands them.

Anyone can be a good defense player; it's much easier to do things *without* the ball to slow you down. Defense is mainly a matter of desire, hustle, agility, energy, and endurance. Sure, there are skills, and we'll discuss them, but defense is more a state of mind. It's playing as though the opponent has *no right to the ball whatsoever*. A good defensive team seems *frantic* to get the ball back. A good defensive player *always* knows where the ball is and *always* looks for a chance to get her hands on it. *Defense wants the ball.* As a parent, you can talk about this concept, repeatedly. If your child gets the message and becomes ball crazy on the floor, it could be the beginning of an excellent ball player. The amount of playing time a kid gets is usually closely associated with his or her all around ability to contribute. A poor defensive player is a liability to the team. A coach can give time to a poor offensive player — they can be hidden better. But nothing upsets coaches more than poor defensive effort. Such players will spend a lot of bench time. There are a number of defensive concepts which need to be ingrained in the minds of young players. Remember, defense is mainly attitude, and if your child gets the idea, it will help him or her immeasurably.

Get back. You can't play defense on the wrong end of the court. Players must get back to their defensive post or assignment *very quickly* when the other team gets the ball. It's one thing to see a tired player come up slowly on offense, it's entirely another to do that on defense. These players will soon find the bench. The time to sprint is when getting back on defense, and many games are lost in this transitional part of the game.

When a player is beaten by a ball handler, he must turn and run to the hoop, try to get in front of the ball handler, and set up to defend again. Remember, a defender can almost always outrun a dribbler. The common error is going directly for the ball, often resulting in a foul. Get back and set up. Catch the player first, then pivot and defend.

Pressure. This is the heart of a good defense. The whole idea is to upset the player with the ball in every possible way. Flailing arms, shaking hand movements, grunts, groans, anything that works to distract the opponent. Don't foul!

The player doesn't need the ball to fake, a defensive player can and should fake body movements. It all serves to confuse the opposition. I've even heard that some players talk to the man they are guarding, to get them riled up, to get them *thinking* too much about what they are doing. I don't encourage the latter, it seems a bit unsportsmanlike. But the player should be encouraged to talk with his body, and the message to be sent is pure confusion. (See Figure 54.)

Keep the action wide, away from the lane. This just makes common sense. The lane area, low and high post, is where the high percentage shots are taken. So we want to always deny the inside route to the dribbler or passer. Force the play to stay wide, along the sideline. The lowest percentage shots are those taken from the corner. They are long, and there is no backboard to give perspective or to give a lucky bank to an errant shot. The idea is to force the ball into the corner if at all possible. Also, the corners act as a

Figure 54
PRESSURE

*Defense is about intimidation. However, don't leave
feet unless ballhandler has used up dribble*

natural trap to a player. They can't go in two directions, so the defense can then bottle up and really frustrate a player. On a baseline drive, we must protect the line and force the ball back up the sideline. There is more help there and a baseline drive is a very high percentage offensive play

Avoid bad fouls. There are times to foul: stopping an otherwise easy lay-up; trying to regain possession in the final minutes of the game; fouling a player who is a terrible foul shooter. Also, there are okay fouls such as when the team has not accumulated many fouls and the player thinks he can take the ball away from a mediocre ball handler, so he reaches in and risks the referee's call.

However, when the team has accumulated five fouls, the other team shoots a one-and-one foul shot. At that point, fouls become very costly. Also, once a player personally accumulates five fouls, he is eliminated from the game. The big players accumulate the most fouls since there is so much action underneath. Young kids tend to get sloppy, and can accumulate fouls rapidly.

It's *very easy* to make body contact underneath. Any movement of the defensive player when attempting to block a shot will usually result in a foul call. Many youth referees will blow the whistle automatically on attempts to block a shot if the players' bodies are close. The best recourse when defending a chippie or short jump shot under the hoop, where bodies are always touching, is just to stand still and erect, hands straight up. (See Figure 55.) I call it *stick 'em up!* It gives up the two points, but puts some pressure on the shot. It also can draw an offensive foul. At the very least, it saves our big man from foul trouble.

Deny. When a player is underneath we want to deny his receiving a pass. Denying players is the cornerstone of defensive strategy today. Most teams use it, particularly when in a zone defense where other defenders can help out against the alley oop pass over the fronting defender. The idea here is that if a player, especially a big player, is in a low post close to the hoop, he will nearly always score if he gets the ball. So, we make sure he *doesn't* get it by

Figure 55
DEFENSE UNDERNEATH

Almost any movement underneath will result in a foul.
So just stand erect, hand straight up

playing *between* him and the ball, or at least by playing to the inside of him and getting an arm around him into the passing lane. This pretty much works only close to the hoop, within 6 feet of it. If it's done farther away, the alley oop pass over the defender is a very effective way to break it. We use fronting only when a player is flashing under the hoop or in a low post. In a zone defense, there is usually another defensive player nearby who can defend if the alley oop gets to the post man. Remember, when denying the ball, we want to keep the hand or body in the *passing lane*. (See Figure 56.)

Switching is another defensive concept. This occurs when a screen or pick releases an offensive player, and another defender needs to take over. This usually is the defender who was guarding the screener. She *switches* to cover the free player.

However, when this occurs, the screener will usually roll into the lane and the other defender must switch also and cover him. We discussed this in the previous chapter, but it bears repeating here. The best way to defend a pick is to *fight through it*. Usually

Figure 56
DENY THE PASS

Underneath, the passing lane must be denied with at least an arm, and preferably with the whole body

other defenders will see the pick as it is being formed and alert the player to be screened so she can step through it or sink behind it. Note that when a player can sink behind the screener, then she can easily cover the screener on a switch. If a switch is to occur, the free defender must call it out loud. This alerts the screened defender to sink back to guard the screener. Otherwise, when fighting through a pick, the idea is to get the leg by the screener and squirm through between her and the ball carrier.

Another tip in defending a screen is for the defender who was guarding the screener to show himself to the ball handler, thus applying some pressure, but keep a close eye on the screener also to see if she rolls to the hoop. Sink back and split the two offensive players, slow them down until help arrives. (See Figure 57.)

The trap is another concept, surrounding a dribbler as soon as she stops dribbling, particularly when along a sideline, and definitely when in any one of the four corners. A second defender comes in right away, particularly if the dribbler looks as though she

Figure 57
DEFENDING THE PICK

Here Renee tries to step through the pick as her teammate "shows" himself to the dribbler

can't get a pass off immediately. Of course, if the player seems to be in the act of or preparing to pass, the trap is off. This play is usually used against a shorter player or one who is not a good ball handler. (See Figure 58.)

DEFENSIVE POSITIONS

We talked earlier about the *triple threat* offensive position. Well, there is also a triple threat defensive position. (See Figure 59.) In this position, a player lines up one long step from the person with the ball. This is just far enough so the defender can reach out and touch the opponent's chest. The triple threat posture allows the defender to move forward, sideways, or upward. Therefore, the player can stop a dribble, a pass, or a shot. Triple threat is simply the position which best allows the player to make any one of those three moves in a split second. The legs are spread and the weight is

Figure 58
THE TRAP

Anytime two defenders can trap a dribbler, the odds
for a turnover increase

balanced on the front half of the feet. The body is low in a crouch, knees bent, waist partially bent. The head is up, always. Hands are out in front of the body, spread just outside shoulder width. Palms are in or up, this is important to reduce fouls. Referees tend to call the downward hand motion a foul, but not an upward motion.

Many coaches teach their players to focus more on the ball handler's belly, since that's the toughest thing to fake. It's much easier to fake the eyes, head, ball, and feet. I think the advice is generally good, conceptually. But a player really needs to stay in touch with the *whole* player. The ball is what we want to get a hand on, so I say we need to keep an eye on it. Stay low and "see" the ball, "see" the whole scene. In fact, we should keep one hand on the ball. I like to see players "track" the ball with the hand closest to it. Wherever the ball is, that hand is as close to it as possible, following it around. Then, if there is a chance for a steal, or a tip, the hand will have started from a closer position. So talk about triple threat,

Figure 59
TRIPLE THREAT DEFENSE

From this position, he can move in any direction, up, right, or left. Also he can defend a shot, pass, or dribble

have a sense for the *center* of the player's action, play the whole player, and keep a hand close to the ball, moving with it.

STEALING THE BALL

In youth basketball, many more passes are stolen than at older ages. The younger child's passes are much softer and are more "telegraphed." A youngster who is *looking to steal*, who thinks about getting the ball will, through observing the opponent's body and eye movements, pick up opportunities to steal. However, most players don't even look for the ball, they don't even think about stealing it. They just don't know how easy it is. It's a state of mind.

Sometimes the passer will let the whole world know where the pass is going. That makes it easy to steal. The stealer wants to set up on the *ball side* of the person he is guarding, and have the hand closest to the ball ready to dart into the passing lane. Tell your child to observe how far it is from her hand to the passing lane between the two offensive players. Most kids don't realize that it's *just a few feet*, a distance they can travel in much less time than it takes the ball to get there. The player *does not have to catch the ball*, it's only necessary to *tip* it away and then scoop it up. The body momentum will bring the player right to its bounce. (See Figure 60.)

The move is a matter of timing. You wait until the passer, often a point or off guard, begins to turn to pass. It's a matter of sensing the right time to move. Coaches will usually say to let the player catch a few passes, and lull them into thinking you are not a threat. Then pick the right time and go. Obviously, if your child has exceptional quickness, if the passer is below average, or if the receiver fails to move *toward* the pass, then steal every time. Watch out, however, because if the steal attempt fails, then the player is free and a score is likely. Pass stealing is like shooting, you must be able to make it much of the time.

The best passes to steal are guard to wing, or wing to corner passes. These passes usually come off regular play patterns, so they can be anticipated better than others. A player can cheat a bit, get ready for the steal when he recognizes the play.

Figure 60
THE STEAL

One of the prettiest plays in basketball is a well timed
steal, yet few kids go for it

REBOUNDING

Rebounding is obviously a skill which is both offensive and defensive, but the fact is that most rebounds are defensive and should be if played properly. Rebounding has much more to do with *position and strength* than with height. Since the defender is usually inside the play, between the man defended and the hoop, the defender is in an excellent position to *box out* or screen that player from the ball. *Boxing out* is a fundamental defensive move which *must be made every time*. The play involves pivoting *toward* the player with the back side, elbows, and legs spread, keeping yourself in between the player and the hoop.

It's important in boxing out to make contact with the player and move with them. The contact will rarely be called a foul unless it is flagrant. Usually, the offensive player is pushing also, so it evens out, and no foul is called. Sometimes, you need to *hold* the player out, other times you just momentarily *bump him* and then *come back* toward the hoop, particularly if you are more than 5 or 6 feet out. Get caught in too far under the hoop — you can do little from there. Don't let your opponent push you under the hoop; get a thigh or hip into the player and hold your ground.

Rebounding is tough business. I loved to get into it underneath in basketball. Rebounders need to be hungry, it helps to be a bit ornery. Underneath is the world of grunts, groans, smacks, and ouches. Players, especially big players, need to understand that they will be intimidating, and they need to assert themselves within the limits of the rules. I'm not suggesting foul play, and never should it to your child. In the long run, it will hurt his own psychological development. But strong aggressive play is definitely needed underneath. If your child is a big player, he must learn to be aggressive underneath. (See Figure 61.)

The rebounder jumps up, preferably straight up to avoid a foul. Don't go over another player who has better position because it's an easy foul to see. Your child should measure her vertical jump. Stand near a wall and reach high, marking the spot. Then leap and see how much higher the hand goes, again marking the wall. The difference is the vertical jump. Boys in high school look for 18 inches, girls 15 inches. Great leapers approach 24 inches. There are drills for improving vertical leap (see Chapter 8).

Catch the ball with two hands. Caution your child against getting into the habit of always tapping the rebound away. A well placed tap against a bigger player may be needed, but always *try* to catch it. Land well, on both feet spread out. Keep the ball high for an overhead outlet pass. If you must bring it down, do so with strength, elbows out, ball into the chest, and pivot quickly. A lot of hands will attack the ball, so be ready and be quick.

Nearly 75% of missed shots will rebound to the opposite side of the hoop, usually at an angle similar to or slightly greater than the shot angle. So if there is freedom and time to move, especially if no teammate is at the opposite side, head or lean that way.

PRESS

Very young teams do not normally press, it's often not allowed. It's just that kids have enough trouble dribbling or passing as it is without being swarmed over. If they were allowed to press at very

Figure 61
REBOUNDING

Players must be aggressive underneath

Jump straight up with strength

Use both hands to grab the ball

Come down with balance

young ages, the ball would rarely get up court. However, by seventh or eighth grade, it is usually allowed. The idea is to apply man-to-man defense for the entire length of the court, right from the in-bounds pass. Usually one defender tries to pressure the inbound passer, and another stays between the other guard and the ball. This usually forces a long, high inbound pass which is susceptible to interception. Just remember that someone has to stay back on defense and others get up court quickly in case the press fails.

MAN-TO-MAN OR ZONE?

I think the rules of basketball should be changed to prohibit zone defenses completely, like in the pros. It's the lazy man's defense. It does not involve as much skill. In a zone, every defender stays in the lane area, low and high post, preventing the inside game. The offense needs to shoot from outside. The kids don't really learn defense, they just clog up the lanes. It's not what the game was meant to be.

Zone defenses are easy to teach, and they are effective, particularly against a good team. If a team does not have good outside shooting, then a zone will work very effectively against them. Also, the often vast skill differences and size differences in third throughseventh graders make a zone suitable, since the zone defense does not allow one player to dominate the game.

The zone defenses are usually a 1-2-2, a 2-1-2, a 1-3-1, or a 2-3. (See Figure 6?) The entire zone formation shifts to the left or to the right depending on where the ball is. Any players underneath are fronted to deny the inside pass. The offense must look to shoot from outside. The weakest part of the zone is the seams, the areas in between the players. Defenders are concentrating on space and not on people, so a quick pass and shot from a seam can catch a defender off guard. This is especially true in a 2-3 zone where the foul line area is usually open. The 1-3-1 stops the center jump shot and allows for good trapping, but its corners and baselines are exposed. The 1-2-2 is the favorite zone defense since it seems to minimize the weakness of other zones.

A man-to-man defense, however, is a more open game, more exciting. Players are pitted against each other, one-on-one, and the

Figure 62
ZONE DEFENSES

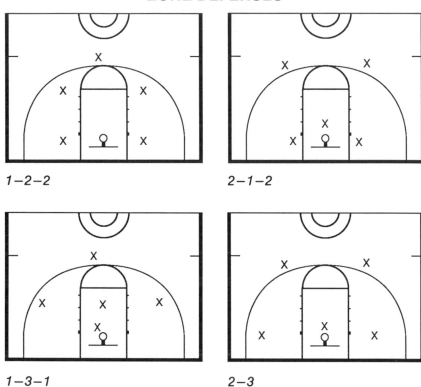

1–2–2   2–1–2

1–3–1   2–3

skill level is more challenging. Kids learn more. It's real defense. It requires better conditioning, better skills, and is a more interesting game to play and to watch. That's why the pros do it that way.

8.

ODDS AND ENDS

WORK WITH YOUR CHILD

As a parent, you should honestly evaluate your child's potential and desire. If he or she is a beginner, then the first objective is to learn the game fundamentals. Go over terminology and concepts. Bring him to a high school, college, or pro game. Sign her up for a clinic. Start by promoting dribbling, lay-ups, and short jump shots.

As your child improves, begin to apply mild pressure during your practice sessions. Don't dominate your child. I used to defend against my sons initially without using my hands. Increase pressure as he can take it, challenge him. Begin to introduce other concepts — give and go, pick and roll, screening, stealing the ball, rebounding. As short jumpers are mastered, move farther out. Practice foul shots.

As your child becomes a decent player, then you can help by concentrating on specific skills. If she's tall, give her low post practice while you defend, again, only aggressively enough to make it a challenge. Forwards should shoot from the corners and wing, and practice baseline drives. Guards needs to practice speed dribbling, so apply open court defensive pressure. Practice snappy passing and outside shooting from above the high post.

Set goals to improve free throw percentage. If he can only make 3 of 20, work to get it to 5, 7, 10, and 15.

BOYS AND GIRLS

Basketball is popular for both boys and girls, and the girls' teams are growing rapidly. It seems to me when viewing girls' games that girls don't seem to practice shooting as much as boys do. Their shot percentages are much lower. If your daughter is interested in playing, concentrate on jump shots — she can be a star very quickly.

The menstrual cycle is usually not a great problem. Modern day pads are quite adequate. Studies show that most women can function as well during their menstrual cycle as otherwise. Of course, everyone is different, but don't let the situation prevent your daughter from playing sports. If your daughter is having a problem, if she is weak or has cramps, give her a note to give to the coach. Usually they will be understanding. Your daughter should wear an athletic bra to protect muscle tone.

CONDITIONING

Basketball is more demanding of endurance than most sports, certainly more than baseball and football. Even in soccer, a player can find a moment to take a breather. Not so in hoops; the motion is nearly always fast. Most coaches will concentrate on improving endurance, and the normal course of practice is quite aerobic. However, jogging and wind sprints are excellent conditioning, and it never hurts to add them to your sessions.

I'd strongly suggest a focus on jumping. Kids can increase their vertical leap, as we discussed in the section on rebounding. Jumping rope is excellent. Some schools have leaper machines. Toe raises are good too.

Hands and fingers need to be strengthened and made more agile. Wrist exercises are helpful. Squeezing the ball for a few moments is fine also. Rolling the ball around the body, between the legs is also good for quickness and agility. Kids also fool around by spinning the ball on the finger. I could never get the hang of it, but my older son is a whiz at it. (See Figure 63.) Overall, agility is partially a state of mind. It helps just to tell your child to *feel* smooth and graceful. It works!

Figure 63
BALL TRICKS

*It doesn't help much on the court, but it shows the
coach you are spending time with the ball*

Muscles are like bubble gum. If you stretch gum quickly it tears
or snaps, but if you stretch it slowly, it expands nicely. No practice
of any kind should begin without some slow jogging (lay-ups are
okay), some jumping jacks (for the ankles), and some general
stretching (upper thigh, trunk, neck). (See Figure 64.)

I don't believe much in weight training for kids under high
school age. The bones are growing rapidly. Calisthenics (wind
sprints, push-ups, sit-ups) are quite sufficient. If you do choose to
do some weight training, the best are toe lifts, partial squats, bench
presses, and rowing exercise. Be sure to include only enough weight
so he or she can do an appropriate number of repetitions without
straining. Go for strength (low weight and high repetitions), not
size (high weight and low repetitions).

INJURIES

No matter how well conditioned a team, injuries can occur any
time. A common injury is a hamstring pull, but these usually don't

Figure 64
WARM-UPS

Jumping jacks are great for loosening up the ankles

Reach forward for the hamstring and lean back for the upper thigh

A partial squat or knee bend will strengthen the knee, and improve jumping

Practice vertical leaps

occur until high school or later ages. Upper leg (groin) strains, shin splints, sprained ankles, bloody noses, sprained wrists and forearms, jammed fingers, and bruises are common to youth basketball. Broken bones are rare, but not rare enough, as my older son learned. With any injury, when in doubt, *see a physician immediately.*

Abrasions usually occur when a child falls and scrapes the arm or the side of the leg. Often, a skid along a gym floor can burn open the skin. A macadam surface opens the skin easily. These are the most likely cuts to get infected. Wash the wound as soon as possible, with soap if it is handy. Apply a dressing when you are able to, the sooner the better. Just put some antiseptic on it. If it gets red, pussy, or red tracks appear, see a physician immediately.

Lacerations are deeper wounds. Unless bleeding is severe, wash the wound, and apply slight pressure with a bandage to stop the bleeding. If severe or deep, seek first aid. Apply pressure and a large bandage. Immediately elevate the wound higher than the heart to slow bleeding. If the bandage gets blood-soaked, apply another on top of it. Don't remove the first one. Care for shock by elevating the legs, unless you suspect a head or neck injury. In this case, don't move the child. If the laceration is minor, a butterfly bandage will hold the skin together. Consult a physician immediately for stitches.

Contusions and bruises occur frequently. Apply ice quickly, after handling any abrasions or lacerations. Ice will arrest internal bleeding and prevent or lessen swelling. Ice is the best first-aid to have available for nearly any swelling from bruises or sprains. *Apply it within minutes,* and much internal damage will be spared.

Sprained ankles or wrists should be immobilized. An ice pack should be applied *immediately.* Act as though there is a fracture until you're sure there is no fracture. Call the ambulance if there is any question in your mind. Get an X-ray to see if there is a break or other damage.

If there is a fracture, immobilize the child completely as soon as possible. There should be no movement at all. Comfort the child, get him warm with coats or blankets, and get medical help. *Do not allow the child to be moved or cared for by anyone who is not medically trained.* If she is in the middle of the floor during a championship game, the game can wait! Insist on this. Permanent damage can result from aggravating a break.

If your child ever falls to the ground unconscious, see if anyone has been trained in first aid. The first move, once it is clear that the child will not respond, is to check for vital signs — breathing and pulse. If either is missing, send for an ambulance and have someone trained administer rescue breathing or CPR (cardio-pulmonary resuscitation). Try to stay calm and let the first-aiders do their job. In all my years of coaching four sports, and playing even more, I've never seen it needed. I hope you won't either.

Finally, *heat exhaustion* can occur during a basketball game. The body gets clammy and pale. Remove the child from the game. Apply cool towels, elevate the feet. If the body temperature is very high and pupils are constricted, you should suspect heat stroke. Call an ambulance and cool him down fast. Care for shock.

Knees are tough injuries. Often the injury will require some sort of arthroscopic surgery to mend cartilage. Modern procedures are quite advanced and simple. Have your child see a knowledgeable sports doctor. Your team's coach or high school athletic director will know one.

Tell your child to play the game safely. Aggressiveness is okay, but be careful not to hurt anyone. Hope that other parents do the same. I play frequently and there are often one or two guys who take chances with each other's health — don't encourage your child to grow up to be one of them.

When injury occurs, insist on rest. I've seen many kids rush back from a sprained ankle, only to have the injury plague them through the years. Don't let it happen! And make sure your child wears an ankle brace from then on. There are excellent ankle braces on the market today. Get one.

The point is that injuries need time to heal right. If you give the time, the future can have many years of sport for your child. If you don't, it could be over already.

HOW TO ACT AT GAMES

The worst thing you can do is go to a basketball game and scream your head off. How often have I seen groups of parents in the stands screaming at the players, giving directions, and generally raising a ruckus. This will only confuse the kids on the floor.

Actually, it is best just to congratulate nice play, and be quiet. The kids on the floor or the coach should be communicating to the player about his options. A lot of screaming parents telling them what to do is just confusing. Don't complain about other players, chances are their parents are nearby. It's really just a game, isn't it?

Be reasonable. Don't confuse the kids. If things are getting loud and hectic, then say nothing. Follow the coach's lead. At young ages, the kids need help, not confusion.

Most important, be positive. Don't criticize anyone, especially your child. Don't take out your frustrations on the kid when he makes a mistake. It embarrasses both of you, and it only teaches the child to play less confidently. I guarantee all kids will make mistakes, for years, and they will not improve if you punctuate mistakes with statements like "What's the matter with you?", "That was stupid!", or "If you don't get going I'll . . ." That kind of talk is disastrous. If you cannot control yourself, then stay home. This may sound tough, but you will do a lot of damage to your child and to your relationship with your child if you don't control anger. Some people just can't keep it in, so avoid damage by staying home. I've seen this problem often, and it really can screw a kid up. If you must yell, then say things like, "Tough D," "Hands up," "Let's go," mainly congratulate a good effort. Never say "Shoot" or "Pass" or anything specific, let the coach call the plays.

HOW TO TREAT THE COACH

First of all, the coach is giving up a lot of time, and deserves a lot of room. If you want to coach, sign up to do so or to help. Show up at practices and offer to help. That earns you the right to have an opinion. Otherwise, be very conservative about offering it.

Second, realize your bias. You are a parent, and you love your child. You may think he deserves to play more, or play another position. But the coach knows a lot more about what kids can do and who has earned playing time. It's unfair for you to ask for more, and unfair to the other kids to suggest, in effect, that one of them should play less. Just work more with your child, so she improves, and she will play more. Coaches want to win, and they usually will give the better players more playing time.

However, coaches need to learn too. And sometimes they are going about matters in quite the wrong way. If this is the case, then gently indicate how you feel. It's important that you think about it a lot, and make sure you know what you are talking about. Question your own bias. But if you feel you can help, offer your opinion about it. Avoid an argument, even a long debate. Make your point, ask the coach to think about it. Indicate you are only trying to help. I would strongly suggest not being argumentative. Say your piece, listen to the coach, then thank her for her time and end it. If you're lucky, the coach will be thankful. However, she may resent your interference and possibly even take it out on your child. If the situation becomes very bad, let your club president or school athletic director know how you feel. But keep in mind that if your child gets in the middle of it, he or she may suffer for it. If the experience is more damaging than good, then remove your child from the team. But remember, think about it, get advice, talk to other parents, avoid being unduly disruptive.

9.

PARENT'S CHECKLIST

Okay, now it's time to get out to the basketball court with your child or team. I find it useful when I coach to have a checklist of things to look for or to say as I work with my kids. A glance at the checklist is a reminder. Repetition of key phrases helps your child concentrate on basics.

DRIBBLING

The best confidence builder for a beginner.

✔ Keep the ball out on the fingers.
✔ Receive the ball, withdraw the hand, cradle it, and pump back out.
✔ Arm and body move with the rhythm of the ball.
✔ Develop both hands.
✔ Head up, eyes front.
✔ Keep ball and body low in traffic.
✔ Shield ball with the body.
✔ Practice head, shoulder, ball, body, pass, and shot fakes.
✔ Use the pivot freely.

PASSING

✔ Critical to good team play.

✔ Know where teammates are.
✔ Use pivot to buy time.
✔ Use two hands.
✔ Spread fingers and rotate fingertips up and into chest area.
✔ Step toward the receiver.
✔ Snap wrists and fingers outward.
✔ Don't broadcast the pass.
✔ Lead the receiver.
✔ Pass to the receiver's chest or outstretched hand.
✔ Pass to the side of receiver opposite the defender.
✔ Overhead pass from a rebound, or to get ball over defender.
✔ Baseball style for long passes.

RECEIVING PASSES

✔ Always know where the ball is.
✔ Don't turn your back to ball handler.
✔ Always want and anticipate a pass.
✔ Move to the pass.
✔ Give a target hand.
✔ Soft hands.
✔ Keep the eyes on the ball.

SHOOTING

The essence of basketball.

✔ Shoot within your range.
✔ Triple threat balance.
✔ Jab step to get free.
✔ Jump straight, off both feet.
✔ Shots start in and come from the legs.
✔ Cradle high.
✔ Shoulders and head square.
✔ Point shooting elbow to the hoop.
✔ Flick wrist, 30 degrees reverse spin, gooseneck finish.
✔ Shoot with only one hand, other hand cradles only.

✔ Achieve reasonable arc.
✔ Soft hands.
✔ Follow the shot.
✔ Always look for open man underneath.
✔ Aim to sit ball on point of hoop closest to you.
✔ Keep options open.
✔ If ball consistently hits back of rim, use more wrist and less forearm.

Lay-ups are great confidence builders.

✔ Claim the lane
✔ Submarine
✔ Take two big steps
✔ Lift knee on shooting hand side
✔ Lay ball up softly
✔ Rotate landing

Foul shots.

✔ Must be constantly practiced
✔ Point shooting side foot at hoop
✔ Be comfortable
✔ Start low
✔ Cradle, raise high, flick and gooseneck
✔ Point elbow at hoop
✔ Square head and shoulders
✔ Extend body fully, up on toes, and hold extension
✔ Post up underneath, fake to one side, and drop step the other way.
✔ Avoid dribbling underneath.

OFFENSE

✔ Look for high percentage shot, in shooter's range, without undue defensive pressure.
✔ Look for post man.
✔ Attack from wing.
✔ Pick and roll.
✔ Give and go.
✔ Don't be too quick to dribble.
✔ Jab and rocker steps.
✔ Shoot when open inside of 12 feet.
✔ Run the offense.
✔ Cut and flash the lane.

DEFENSE

✔ Get back on defense quickly.
✔ Pressure.
✔ Confuse the ball handler.
✔ Keep the ball wide, away from the lane.
✔ Avoid bad fouls, especially underneath.
✔ Deny to plays underneath.
✔ Fight through or sink behind screen.
✔ Switch and slow down pick and roll until help arrives.
✔ Trap when possible.
✔ Triple threat.
✔ Look for steals — track ball with ball-side hand.
✔ Rebound, box out, catch with two hands.

INDEX

Other Books of Interest

Home Construction/Repair

Home/Family

The Christmas Lover's Handbook, $14.95
Clutter's Last Stand, $10.95
Confessions of a Happily Organized Family, $10.95
Confessions of an Organized Homemaker, $10.95
Conquering the Paper Pile-Up, $11.95
The Genealogist's Companion & Sourcebook, $16.95
The Greatest Gift Guide Ever, 2nd Edition, $8.95
How to Conquer Clutter, $10.95
How to Get Organized When You Don't Have the Time, $10.95
How to Have a Big Wedding on a Small Budget, $12.95
The Big Wedding on a Small Budget Planner & Organizer, $12.95
How to Have a Fabulous, Romantic Honeymoon on a Budget, $12.95
Into the Mouths of Babes: A Natural Foods Cookbook for Infants and Toddlers, $6.95
Is There Life After Housework?, $10.95
It Doesn't Grow on Trees, $2.95
It's Here . . . Somewhere, $10.95
Kids, Money & Values, $10.95
Make Your House Do the Housework, $12.95
The Melting Pot Book of Baby Names, 2nd Ed., $9.95
The Organization Map, $12.95
A Parent's Guide to Teaching Music, $7.95
A Parent's Guide to Band and Orchestra, $7.95
A Parent's Guide to Teaching Art: How to Encourage Your Child's Artistic Talent and Ability, $5.95
Raising Happy Kids on a Reasonable Budget, $10.95
Slow Down . . . And Get More Done, $11.95
Step-by-Step Parenting, Revised & Updated, $9.95
Streamlining Your Life, $11.95
Unpuzzling Your Past: A Basic Guide to Genealogy, 2nd Ed., $12.95

Sports/Coaching

The Art of Doubles: Winning Tennis strategies, $14.95
Baseball Chronicles: An Oral Historyof Baseball Through the Decades, $16.95
Baseball Fathers, Baseball Sons: From Orator Jim to Cal, Barry, and Ken . . . Every One a Player, $13.95
Baseball's All-Time Dream Team, $12.95
The Complete Guide & Resource to In-Line Skating, $12.95
The Downhill Skiing Handbook, $17.95
Intelligent Doubles: The Sensible Approach to Better Doubles Play, $9.95
Intelligent Tennis, $9.95
The Joy of Walking: More Than Just Exercise, $9.95
The Name of the Game: How Sports Talk Got That Way, $8.95
Never Too Old to Play Tennis . . . And Never Too Old to Start, $12.95
A Parent's Guide to Coaching Football, $7.95
A Parent's Guide to Coaching Baseball, $7.95
A Parent's Guide to Coaching Basketball, $7.95
The Parent's Guide to Coaching Hockey, $8.95
The Parent's Guide to Teaching Skiing, $8.95
A Parent's Guide to Coaching Tennis, $7.95
A Parent's Guide to Coaching Soccer, $8.95
A Practical Self-Defense Guide for Women, $16.95
Spinning: A Complete Guide to the World of Cycling, $14.95
The Scuba Diving Handbook: A Complete Guide to Salt and Fresh Water Diving, $19.95
Underwater Adventures: 50 of the World's Greatest!, $19.95

Young Readers

But Everyone Else Looks so Sure of Themselves: A Guide to Surviving the Teen Years, $9.95
The Junior Tennis Handbook: A Complete Guide to Tennis for Juniors, Parents & Coaches, $12.95
The Kids' Almanac of Professional Football, $8.95
Market Guide for Young Artists and Photographers, $12.95
Market Guide for Young Writers, 2nd Ed., $16.95
Roots for Kids: A Genealogy Guide for Young People, $7.95
What Would we do Without You? A Guide to Volunteer Activities for Kids, $6.95
With Secrets to Keep, $12.95
Woman of Independence: The Life of Abigail Adams, $5.95
Young Person's Guide to Becoming a Writer, $8.95

For a complete catalog of Betterway Books write to the address below. To order, send a check or money order for the price of the book(s). Include $3.00 postage and handling for 1 book, and $1.00 for each additional book. Allow 30 days for delivery.

Betterway Books
1507 Dana Avenue, Cincinnati, Ohio 45207
Credit card orders call TOLL-FREE
1-800-289-0963
Quantities are limited; prices subject to change without notice.